THE
TUPAMARO
GUERRILLAS

THE TUPAMARO GUERRILLAS

Maria Esther Gilio

Translated by
ANNE EDMONDSON

Introduction by
ROBERT J. ALEXANDER

Saturday Review Press · New York

Library of Congress Catalog Card Number: 72–79051
ISBN 0–8415–0211–0

Saturday Review Press
230 Park Avenue
New York, New York 10017

PRINTED IN THE UNITED STATES OF AMERICA

Dedicated to those who died

Jorge Salerno
Mario Rovaina
Carlos Flores
Fernan Pucurull
Indalecio Olivera
Alfredo Cultelli
Ricardo Zabalza

Contents

Foreword

Maria Esther Gilio's excellent and moving book has been written at exactly the right moment in history, when South America, long ignored and misunderstood by the world, is beginning for the first time to be seen as a politically amorphous and disturbing shape looming through the mists of romantic nonsense created in people's minds by sheer distance and the barrier of the Monroe Doctrine, whereby long ago the USA assumed the self-appointed role of protector – or exploiter – of the conglomeration of the then newly independent Latin American nations.

There are enormous differences between one South American country and another, which is not surprising considering the diversity of climate and terrain, ranging from deepest jungle to the icy wastes of Patagonia dipping into Antarctica, and from the rarefied cold of the Andean plateaux to the lush fertile coastal lands. Every degree of human endeavour is represented, from the stone-age tribesmen of the jungles of Northern Brazil, through the strange relics of ancient peoples living on the high plateaux, to the ultra-civilised populations, of predominantly European blood, in the larger, richer countries in the South, where art, literature and science flourish on a par with the best in modern Europe.

Uruguay belongs in this latter category of nations. She has a fine tradition of democracy and was the first South American welfare state, but, like most of the Latin American countries, she has been economically trammelled from the beginning, first by the European countries and later by the USA. She is not so much underdeveloped as economically stagnant and regressing unhappily into a dark age of repression.

It is these repressive conditions in the country that have given rise to the Tupamaros and brought Uruguay into the limelight momentarily through the kidnapping and subsequent release of the British Ambassador, and it is fitting that at this stage the case for the Tupamaros should be presented fairly to the world: not as vindication for the kidnapping of Sir Geoffrey Jackson, but rather as an indictment of a régime which has driven ordinary men and women to resort to such extreme measures. Miss Gilio has done this admirably.

Her book is factual, wholly authentic and deeply human. It consists mainly of straightforward journalistic reporting. It is a book written by the people of Uruguay through Miss Gilio. The clear tones of children, solemn intonations of priests, voices of the old, the imprisoned, the hopeless, the sick and insane, the unscrupulous, the cruel and the youthfully buoyant all ring through its pages.

Some of the interviews are funny, some heartrending, some quite horrible. Miss Gilio herself says that in her efforts to report truthfully, without sentimentality or bias, she felt she was sinking into professional hardness which blinded her to the pain and suffering she witnessed. It is a most revealing work from which there emerges a picture of a country struggling with itself.

How and when the National Liberation Movement actually started will perhaps never be told. It is of fairly recent origin and was probably initiated by a small group of intellectuals and professionals appalled by government inadequacy in face of national economic ruin and the ever-increasing repression practised by the Pacheco régime. The name 'Tupamaro', a Guarani Indian word for a large, ungainly and noisy bird, could be a clue. Noisy birds are difficult to suppress and the Tupamaros could, like the geese who saved Rome, perform a useful service for their country. It is also said that the Tupamaros have called themselves after the Uruguayan gauchos who rebelled against the Spaniards in the War of Independence in the last century: they themselves took the name Tupamaro from Tupac Amaru, an Inca hero of the Peruvian resistance of the eighteenth century.

As an urban guerrilla the Tupamaros are not quite like any other guerrilla. One could almost call them gentlemen amateurs. Their activities are basically patterned on the Brazilian urban guerrilla movement as set out in Carlos Marighela's book *For the Liberation of Brazil* (published by Penguin). This is the Urban Guerrilla's Manual. But the Tupamaros are not nearly as ruthless, *so far*. Again although Fidel Castro and, more especially, Che Guevara are greatly admired, not to say revered, and Guevara's teachings are taken to heart, the Cuban Revolution and the exploits of Guevara in Bolivia (where he was killed on 8 October 1967) were open wars of liberation, with full-time guerrilla groups, working on an all-out campaign, not members of the community carrying out a swift exploit and then slipping back behind the typewriter or lathe.

The Movement's early activities as a revolutionary body may well have passed unrecorded by the authorities, but by 1967 and early 1968 the word 'Tupamaros' was something to be taken seriously.

I like to feel that those first initiators thought of themselves as the conscience of Uruguay, working in secret to expose malpractice in government departments, big business and finance, and seeking to redress injustice where possible. There is throughout an endearing element of Robin Hood or 'The Four Just Men' in their exploits, and this aura undoubtedly caught the public imagination so that the Movement grew with unprecedented rapidity. As Miss Gilio says in her Introduction, not only was the whole of Latin America surprised at the appearance and swift spread of the insurgent movement in Uruguay, but the Uruguayans themselves were taken by surprise.

An important feature of the Tupamaros, as revealed in the book, is this extreme secrecy which pervades the Movement. The members are divided into small groups or cells and are only acquainted with the few members in their own group. The secrecy would appear to be as strictly observed as, for instance, the masonic code, and there is apparently no password or sign for identifying other members. The groups work in strict isolation under the command of an officer whose range of contacts presumably is equally limited. Even in a major action such as the taking of Pando, the identifying badge was a handkerchief worn round the arm, nothing more, a simple part of everybody's clothing which, once the job was done, could be taken off and put back in the pocket.

This system is probably the Movement's greatest strength as even under torture – to which captured Tupamaros are frequently subjected – the unfortunate man or woman is quite unable to give more than very limited information. The system also serves in cutting down to a minimum the possibility that greed could lead a member to betray important secrets in return for a large bribe.

The strange double life which this secrecy necessarily imposes must be psychologically burdensome, a fact which Miss Gilio mentions in this book. Urban guerrillas strike and then melt back into their home or work environment, disappearing more completely than could ever be possible for guerrillas working in wild, open country. This means that office colleagues, workmates, parents, wives, husbands, children must all be kept in the dark.

The awful secret cannot be shared lest when the police come pounding on the door somebody should break down from sheer terror. It also means that nobody knows who is or is not a Tupamaro. Nobody can be sure whether a member of their family or staff is involved. The dreamy-eyed daughter with the thick blonde hair, the studious, respectful, smartly-dressed son, the dull obsequious clerk, the irascible accountant, the sensible housewife, the cheeky milk-boy, they all could be – and probably are – Tupamaros. That secret hidey-hole at the top of the cupboard where Mum discovered her son's treasure trove of pornographic magazines could now well hold a sub-machine-gun, and the gorgeous blonde probably finds that the revolvers in her mattress make her bed lumpy.

Only when an active member is caught by the police during an exploit or a raid does his or her identity become definitely known, though they may be suspected, and it is obvious from the book that the 'soldiers' who are the ones most likely to be caught are usually drawn from the working class or petite bourgeoisie. The 'officer' types may come from the professional and perhaps even the ruling classes, it is presumed, not because of class distinction but simply, as emerges from the book, because enterprise and authoritative qualities, indispensable in a movement of this nature, do not attract the attention of the police when displayed by the richer, better-educated members of the community, whereas trade-union leaders, student leaders and so on are usually earmarked as potential trouble-makers and swept up at the first excuse.

The military terms I use are not mine. Military references appear frequently in the interviews with captured Tupamaros and they evidently think of themselves in a military context. The attack on Pando for instance was handled as a precise military operation.

There is no doubt that the Tupamaros enjoy a great deal of public support though this may not always be overt from fear of consequences. This comes through in practically every chapter of the book, the support sometimes appearing from very unlikely quarters. It is tempting to think that if there is so much public support for the Movement and its aims and objectives, the members have only to establish themselves openly as a political party to canvass support at the polls and operate legitimately. But the matter has to be seen in the context of a repressive régime, where any such hope would be naïve.

In her Introduction Miss Gilio points out that from being a

democracy with liberal traditions Uruguay has, by force of circumstances and creeping bankruptcy, changed into a harsh oligarchy.
As one of the interviewees pungently says, 'democracy's all right
during the good times, it doesn't work when things are bad', and
it is not only in Uruguay that when things go wrong the public cry
out loudly for 'tougher measures, bring back the birch' – or hanging – or whatever. For a time the public longs to hide behind a
tough government, relapsing into childish dependence and security,
hoping that 'strong men' will magically conjure away all the
country's troubles. When they pluck up their courage to open
their eyes they find it is too late and the monster they invoked is
firmly installed and not to be ousted. The enlightened few who
may have kept their heads and have plans for helping the country
find it difficult, if not impossible, to operate openly. If the Tupamaros leaders tried to establish a political party they would probably be picked off one by one and their supporters persecuted or
simply frightened into denying them.

Some may say that Miss Gilio's book is one-sided and gives a
sentimental view of a group who are no more than a gang of thugs,
kidnappers and murderers. In reply I would point out that the
Press in neighbouring Argentina has reported the various incidents
much as they are reported in the book, and the serious Argentine
papers cannot be accused of bias or special sympathy for the Tupamaros.

From the point of view of violence, it is clear that although the
Tupamaros accept violence as a legitimate means to an end they
do not use it as a first resort nor indiscriminately. This is fully
borne out by the figures showing that, in general, there is very little
bloodshed and that the Tupamaros usually suffer heavier losses
than they inflict. It would, however, be a mistake to take this as a
sign of weakness when one considers that there are probably Tupamaros in practically every organisation or institution. The damage
they could do if undisciplined can easily be imagined.

In the taking of Pando alone, had there been uncontrolled thug-
gery or even plain vindictiveness the toll could have been enormous.
The fact that the whole affair was handled like an Errol Flynn film,
full of heroics, charm and enchantment, sets the Tupamaros on a
separate plane in the realms of guerrilla warfare.

The question of the kidnappings is delicate and uncertain ground.
The killing of the kidnapped American inspires loathing. But the

Tupamaros say they did not kill him. They claim that he was a CIA spy who had become useless to his own side and was killed by his own masters. On their record this could be true.

The kidnapping of the British Ambassador is difficult to judge objectively. In the Guerrilla's Manual, kidnapping of important people including foreign diplomats, for bargaining purposes, is legitimate. The Tupamaros had one hundred and eleven of their members in prison and they wanted to exchange Sir Geoffrey Jackson for these prisoners. In the end they engineered the prisoners' escape themselves, and then voluntarily released the British Ambassador. The Tupamaros have been silent on how they captured him and about his period of captivity. It is only from Sir Geoffrey's own comments in his Press interviews that it would appear that his captors were young men and that they hoped, and one would almost say prayed, that they would not have to kill him (which they would have done if the police had found his hiding place). I confess that after spending eight months in captivity I would not have been a quarter as charitable to my captors as Sir Geoffrey was in his subsequent interviews. Only he can know what they said to him and what he felt. But in mitigation – now that he is mercifully safe – it could be said that they were desperate men. It is many centuries since England has had to face the sort of appalling internal situation which prevails today in Uruguay so it is difficult for us to find excuses for such an act. I say this with my English personality, but I have another personality, a South American one. I was born in one South American country, inherited half my ancestry from another and lived for twenty years in a third. In my youth I have had my share of revolution. I have had to nip smartly across the street under the tossing heads of the Coracero horses waiting to charge, and have ducked into shop doors to avoid a hail of bullets. As I translated Miss Gilio's book I became deeply involved. I listened with her to those voices, thrilled at the exploits of the Tupamaros and metaphorically humped a machine-gun on their behalf.

I hope as the readers accompany Miss Gilio through her many interviews they too will feel involved and perhaps understand in some small measure the urgent need felt by the repressed to fight back with whatever means are at hand.

Anne Edmondson

THE
TUPAMARO
GUERRILLAS

Introduction by
Robert J. Alexander

This book recounts the tragedy of a nation. During the first three or four decades of this century, Uruguay was a model for most of the rest of Latin America. Since World War II, however, this country, which was once labeled a "Utopia," has experienced an economic, social, and political crisis that has intensified with each year. The nation's leaders at first refused to recognize that there even was a crisis, and when they finally realized the seriousness of the situation, they seemed paralyzed, unable to resolve it. As this volume indicates, they have responded principally with repression.

The Early Reforms

During the first decade of the twentieth century, Uruguay began to experience a series of fundamental changes that made it a pioneer in economic, social, and political reform. For example, the government launched a program of economic nationalism. The docks were nationalized, and a government monopoly on the production of gasoline, alcohol products, and their derivatives was set up. The government was also given a monopoly on insuring employers for workmen's compensation, and extensive participation in other kinds of insurance. A portion of the banking industry was also put under state control. Similarly, the provision of electric power and telephone and telegraph service was made a government function. Subsequently, right after World War II, the country's foreign-owned railroads were nationalized, as were some of the packinghouses, which provided a large part of the nation's foreign exchange.

Thus, the influence of foreign capital in the Uruguayan economy was reduced substantially below what is characteristic of most of the other Latin American countries. However, it is also true that the national economy remained very sensitive to changes in the market for its principal export products—meat, hides, and wool. Britain remained the largest purchaser of Uruguayan products; West Germany, Brazil, and Argentina were its other major trading partners.

Economic nationalism was only one of the policies adopted in the early decades of this century. Far-reaching labor legislation was put on the books, and a comprehensive social security system was established, providing not only workmen's compensation, but also health insurance and pensions, covering the great majority of the population.

Although the governments of the period encouraged the growth of trade unionism and collective bargaining, they did not seek to exercise close control over the unions. Legal recognition was not necessary for a union to engage in collective bargaining. In this, too, Uruguay differed sharply from most of the other Latin American countries, which, although they recognized unions as legitimate, sought to impose more or less strict controls on them.

Uruguay was also a pioneer in spreading mass education. Unlike those in most Latin American countries, the Uruguayan school system was not confined to the large cities, but was also extended to the countryside. For instance, if one had traveled in buses through the rural areas during the years immediately after World War II, one would have found that many of the passengers were school-children being taken to and from the country schools.

Political democracy was another of the achievements of the early decades of this century. The change of governments through the process of elections became the standard in Uruguay. Widespread political freedom existed, and a variety of political parties functioned openly. Uruguay is one of the few Latin American countries in which the Communist Party has been allowed to function legally, virtually from its very beginning.

Political Structure

Two traditional parties have tended to dominate national politics. These are the Partido Colorado (Red Party) and the Partido Blanco (White Party), also known as the Partido Nacionalista (Nationalist Party). These parties originated during the early years of national independence, forming around the leaders of the independence struggles.

The Colorados and Blancos historically have represented different elements in national life. The strength of the Colorados has been centered in the capital city, Montevideo, where they have had the support of merchants and artisans; the Blancos have tended to receive the loyalty of most people in the interior, especially the landlords, but also those who have worked for them.

The continued dominance of the two traditional parties has been facilitated by a unique electoral system, adopted early in the century. This has allowed a form of simultaneous primary and general elections. Each party can put up as many candidates for president as it wants, each backed by a particular faction. The decision as to which party wins then depends on the total number of votes received by the rival candidates within each party. The final victory goes to the factional leader within the majority party who has won the most votes.

This system has prevented the splintering of the two major parties. Although factions have been formed within each of them, these generally have remained within the broader Colorado and Blanco structure, and at election time the votes of all rival factions have served to increase the total vote of the two major parties.

However, smaller parties did develop outside of the Colorado and Blanco framework. For several decades the most important of these have been the Unión Cívica (Civic Union), now the Partido Demócrata Cristiano (Christian Democratic Party); the Socialists; and the Communists.

The Unión Cívica was a Catholic-oriented party. Until after World War II, it generally supported the privileges and general position of the Catholic Church within Uruguayan society. However, after World War II, it was affected by the growth of Christian Democracy in Europe and Latin America, and by the early 1960s, a majority of its members considered themselves to be of that orientation. They therefore rechristened the party the Partido Demócrata Cristiano. A conservative minority withdrew from the party, and the PDC moved increasingly to the Left.

The first Socialist Party of Uruguay was founded in 1910 by the poet Emilio Frugoni. During World War I it gained widespread influence in the labor movement. When the party decided to join the Communist International in 1922, a minority led by Frugoni withdrew to re-establish the Socialist Party. During the next three and a half decades it was a fairly orthodox Social Democratic Party, belonging to the Second International. However, in the late 1950s it began to move quickly to the Left, soon coming to consider itself Marxist-Leninist and to the Left of the Communist Party.

3

The founders of the Tupamaro movement seem to have gained their first political experience in the Socialist Party.

During the 1930s the re-established Socialist Party began to regain influence in the labor movement. The Communist Party contested Socialist control over the labor movement during the first decade after joining the Comintern and during the 1940s tended to be the dominant party in the movement. In the 1950s, Communist influence declined drastically, but this trend was reversed in the early 1960s, and by the end of the decade the Communists dominated almost the whole labor movement.

The three minority parties have tended to receive about 20 percent of the total vote in succeeding elections from the 1930s on. Almost half of this has been cast for the Unión Cívica (now the Partido Demócrata Cristiano), while the Socialists and Communists have split the other half. Generally, as Socialist influence has risen, Communist influence has declined, and vice versa.

The Influence of José Batlle

The transformation of Uruguay from the backward and politically chaotic country that it had been in the nineteenth century, into the progressive democracy that it subsequently became, was largely the work of José Batlle y Ordóñez. The son of a former president, he served as president from 1903 to 1907 and again from 1911 until 1915. He was largely responsible for launching the program of economic nationalism; he also sponsored the beginning of mass education and launched the labor and social legislation that came to distinguish Uruguay from the other Latin American countries.

Batlle was also a firm believer in political democracy. He sought the enactment of a new constitution, which was finally adopted in 1917, two years after he left office for the second time. This constitution separated Church and State, and brought about other reforms.

Batlle sought to bring about the establishment of a Swiss type of "collegiate" government, in which the executive branch would be headed by a nine-man National Executive Council, in place of the traditional president. He had several reasons for doing this.

Certainly one major objective of Batlle was to lessen the possi-

4

bility that the Uruguayan executive might establish a dictatorship. However, he also had in mind a device to discourage the opposition Partido Blanco, which had been out of power since the 1860s, from trying to overthrow the government by force. The Batlle collegiate-government scheme provided for six members of the National Executive Council to come from the majority party and three from the minority one. Thus, the Blancos not only would have representation in the legislature, but would also participate in the activities of the executive branch.

Batlle was only partially successful in getting the collegiate form of executive established. It did not become fully operational until almost a quarter of a century after his death.

Batlle's influence continued long after his demise in 1929. In fact, the members of the Partido Colorado, who continued to rule the country until 1958, tended to ride along on Batlle's record and his ideas. They, like most Uruguayans, tended to believe that virtually all of the country's problems had been resolved during the Batlle period, and refused to recognize new ones that had begun to develop with increasing rapidity after World War II.

The Nature of Uruguay's Crisis

The growing crisis had many roots. One of the most fundamental was the failure of Uruguayan grazing to keep pace with technological developments in other parts of the world. New grasses, fertilizers, and other improvements were not introduced. The productivity of grazing, therefore, did not increase, although costs did. The income accruing to the country did not increase while the need for foreign exchange did.

During World War II, the Uruguayan government stimulated the growth of wheat farming, in response to the attempt of the Perón government in Argentina to refuse grain shipments to Uruguay in order to punish the Uruguayans for giving refuge to Perón's opponents. However, wheat was produced in Uruguay at a high cost, so a subsidy was necessary after World War II in order to allow it to compete with imported grain.

A somewhat similar situation faced the country's manufacturing industries. These had grown rapidly during World War II, when the country was cut off from imports. However, Uruguayan manu-

5

factures, too, were high-priced, as a result of the small size of the national market.

Other problems originated in the Batlle reforms. For one thing, the social security system was constantly amplified, insofar as its benefits were concerned. It inevitably reached the point where it placed a severe strain on the whole economy. This was in large part due to the organizational structure of the system. Instead of consisting of a single fund, it was divided into more than thirty different funds, each covering different groups of workers. It became possible for a worker who had several jobs to "retire" under the social security system of one of these, draw a pension, and continue to work in his other jobs. Tens and perhaps hundreds of thousands of people did so. The situation was complicated by the short period of work required for retirement—sometimes only twenty years—and by the fact that social security benefits from a single fund were not sufficient to provide a person with an adequate living. This problem is underscored in the numerous interviews contained in this book.

Another problem arose from Batlle's extension of government activities into a variety of fields. One result was that half or more of the country's gainfully employed came to work for the government. This would have been no handicap to the economy were it not for the fact that virtually all government employees also held at least one other job. They spent only a few short hours each workday in their government positions, worked another relatively short period in a civilian job (or another government one), and sometimes spent more time on a third one. Although highly inefficient in all three posts, they, nonetheless, needed them in order to earn a satisfactory income. This problem, too, is reflected in the pages that follow, in the interviews with people in government-run hospitals and asylums, where those interviewed complain frequently of the scanty visits made by doctors and other trained personnel, too busy with other work.

All of these problems contributed to yet another major problem: the rising inflation. This began in the 1950s and by the middle 1960s had achieved galloping proportions. It resulted in large part from the government's unbalanced budget. The deficit was made up by borrowing from the social security funds, and from the Central Bank. The difference between the government's expenditures and the amount it took in in taxes brought constant pressure on the price level. Inflation is also referred to frequently in the pages that follow.

Governmental Irresponsibility

Little was done during the quarter of a century after World War II to come to grips with these problems. Indeed, they were hardly even recognized to exist by the regimes that ruled in that period.

Many things would have been necessary to solve the problems facing the nation. Reorganization of the grazing industry, with the adoption of modern techniques and the return of wheat land to grazing, was certainly essential. In addition, steps were necessary to expand the economy, and this could have been done only by developing industries complementary to those of Uruguay's two neighbors, Brazil and Argentina.

A number of such complementary measures were possible. For instance, Uruguay possesses extensive iron deposits in the north. Although Uruguay's own market is not sufficient to justify an iron and steel industry of any consequence, Argentina has a steel industry within easy reach of the Uruguayan deposits. It would have been possible to build installations to produce pig iron at the site of these iron reserves; the pig iron could then have been shipped to the Argentine plant at San Nicolás for processing into steel.

Successive Uruguayan governments have refused to work out agreements such as this with their more powerful neighbors. After their experiences with Perón, they did not want the economy to become dependent upon that of Argentina. They felt much the same way with regard to Brazil.

Other basic reforms were necessary. A reorganization of the economy, to allow transfer of a large number of government workers to private employment, and perhaps vice versa, was essential. A rational organization of the Uruguayan economy would require that workers, whether employed by the government or private firms, work a full day, and therefore receive a full day's pay. Both the government services and the private sector would then be more efficient.

The social security system also required reorganization. A system whereby a single social security fund could provide adequate

7

services to all those registered with it would eliminate much over-head and probably cost a good deal less than the unwieldy system that had grown up during and after Batlle's period.

However, relatively little was done by any administration to deal with the growing crisis. The Nationalist governments of the 1960s did begin a modest program for replanting the grazing area with new kinds of more productive grasses. The government of President Jorge Pacheco undertook the beginnings of a reorganiza-tion of the social security system. But these efforts were trifling compared with what was needed and came too late in any case.

For many years another of Batlle's innovations complicated at-tempts to do something about the country's problems. This was the collegiate system of government, which had finally been adopted by popular referendum in 1951. As a result, nine men, in-stead of a single president, held the executive power jointly during the next four administrations. This led to a massive evasion of re-sponsibility by the members of the succeeding National Executive Councils. The single-president system was not restored until the election of 1966.

The upshot was that there was a constant deterioration of popular levels of living and of public services of all kinds. This is reflected in the interviews in this book, in which prisoners, attendants in mental institutions, and other people interviewed compare the situation in their organizations in the late 1960s with the much better conditions that had existed a decade or more before.

Growing Discontent

In the face of this situation, popular discontent began to rise. The first clear evidence of this came in 1958 when, for the first time in nearly one hundred years, the Partido Blanco, or Nationalist Party, defeated the Partido Colorado. For the following eight years, the National Executive Council was controlled by the Naciona-listas. However, because of their failure to handle the rapidly mounting crisis, the Colorados won once again.

Another indication of mounting political tension was the grow-ing factionalism within the traditional political parties. There had been several groups within the Partido Colorado ever since the second Batlle Administration, but the number grew markedly in

8

the 1960s. In addition, the Partido Blanco also splintered into half a dozen different groups. Within both traditional parties, the factions tended to range from Left to Right, although the extremes of these positions were not represented.

Still other evidence of discontent was the situation in the organized labor movement. For fifteen years after World War II, Communist influence in the unions declined. However, during the 1960s the Confederación Sindical Uruguaya, consisting of unions controlled by various parties, declined and finally disappeared, while the Communists organized a new Central Nacional de Trabajadores, which by the end of the decade had the overwhelming majority of the unions in its ranks.

Perhaps most Uruguayans have been more bewildered than angry about what has happened to them in the last decade and a half. Most of them have been used to a relatively high standard of living and have been at a loss to understand what it is that has gone wrong with their nation and its economy. They have felt very frustrated and have tended to hit out in a variety of ways at those they think responsible for the quandary they have found themselves in.

Until recently, the natural reaction of the Uruguayans has been to strike back through the ballot box. This they did in 1958, when they ousted the Colorados after a century in power; they did it again in 1966 when they restored the Colorados to power. Many of them did it once again in 1971, when they voted for the left-wing Frente Amplio.

The Tupamaros

The Tupamaros are undoubtedly other evidence of the growing discontent and unhappiness of the Uruguayan people. Although they are relatively few in number, they have undoubtedly gained sympathy among sizable elements of the Uruguayan population. As the incidents related in this volume correctly indicate, the Tupamaros have found large numbers of people willing to give them refuge, cover their tracks, and otherwise aid their attacks on the status quo.

The Tupamaro movement originated in the early 1960s—the author of this book mentions the year 1962—with a group of left-wing members of the Socialist Party. For a number of years the

9

Socialist Party, which before the mid-1950s had been a Second International group, had been moving to the Left. This was particularly noticeable after the victory of Fidel Castro in 1959, which aroused great enthusiasm in the party's ranks.

However, the Socialist Party generally stayed within the electoral framework of Uruguayan politics. Those supposedly led by Roberto Sendic, who broke with the party to form the Tupamaros, did not believe that the electoral road was the way to power. Rather, they believed in direct action, leading to a violent revolution, as the major road to the socialist revolution. That they did not rule out elections completely was shown by their support of the Frente Amplio in 1971, but that they did not feel elections were the principal road to be followed is amply evident in this book.

The Tupamaros in the Latin American Extreme Left

The Tupamaros have in the last half dozen years become somewhat of a model for the extreme Left in Latin America. They have become the almost classic example of the urban guerrilla.

However, the Tupamaros are by no means the first group to attempt this particular method of coming to power. The guerrilla war that plagued Venezuela between 1962 and 1966 started as principally an urban operation. During its first two years, it was characterized by kidnappings of prominent foreigners, bank robberies, random killing of policemen, burning of foreign-owned enterprises, and other similar operations. Only after the election of 1963—in which over 90 percent of the eligible voters cast their ballots, in spite of guerrilla threats against those who attempted to do so, and elected a member of the governing party to succeed President Romulo Betancourt—resulted in a severe defeat for the urban guerrillas, did they turn principally to rural guerrilla activities.

Brazilian urban guerrillas also preceded the Tupamaros. Although the political groups resorting to this kind of activity after the military coup d'etat of April 1, 1964, were numerous, the most important figure to appear among these was Carlos Marighella. A former leader of the pro-Moscow Communist Party and a onetime member of the Chamber of Deputies, Marighella became the ideologist of the Brazilian urban guerrilla movement. As this volume indicates, the Tupamaros have tended to regard him as the principal theoretician of their particular kind of political movement.

In the late 1960s urban guerrilla activities superseded similar operations in the countryside as the principal focus of the most extreme elements in the Latin American Left. In large part, this shift in emphasis came about as a result of the failure of the rural guerrilla activities, which found their major inspiration in the writings of Ernesto "Che" Guevara and Régis Debray.

Guevara was the author of the so-called foco theory of revolutionary warfare, and Debray elaborated this theory in a form that was accepted more or less as the official position of the Castro regime insofar as the road to power was concerned. In capsule form, the foco theory argues, first, that a group of young middle-class people from the city can go into the countryside and organize a center ("foco") of guerrilla activity, which is first directed at destroying governmental authority in a limited area. Second, the foco theory argues that it is not necessary to prepare the ground politically among the peasants for a rural guerrilla movement to succeed. Also, it is not necessary for the movement to be led by a political party since, the theory argues, this will emerge from the guerrilla army once its victory has been assured.

The foco theory took many defeats during the 1960s. It failed to prove true in Venezuela, Guatemala, Argentina, Peru, and Colombia. It had its most spectacular defeat in Bolivia, where Che Guevara himself undertook to lead a small rural guerrilla army (mainly composed of Cubans and other non-Bolivians) to victory. He was killed after being captured in October, 1967.

The rural guerrilla movements enjoyed the strong and open support of the Castro regime. However, the connection of the urban guerrillas with Fidel is not so clear. It is true that the members of the Movimiento de Izquierda Revolucionaria of Chile, which until the election of Salvador Allende as president concentrated principally on urban guerrilla activities, were self-proclaimed disciples of Fidel, but his influence is not so clear-cut in other areas. The principal urban guerrilla element in Argentina, the Partido Revolucionario de Trabajadores, is composed of Trotskyites, who support Castro but do not draw their principal inspiration from him or his regime.

The connection of the Tupamaros with Castro is also more or less vague. Undoubtedly, Fidel is for them an inspiration, but he is only one of many. As already indicated, the Tupamaros have looked doctrinally to the Brazilian Carlos Marighella.

It is yet to be proven that urban guerrilla activity will be any more successful than rural guerrilla activity has been. Whether the Tupamaros will be able to come to power will depend in large part on the ability of the more traditional elements in Uruguayan politics to deal with the problems that plague Uruguay and create the circumstances that generate a considerable degree of popular support, or at least sympathy, for the Tupamaros.

Introduction

Uruguay, once known as 'The Switzerland of America' and 'The Picture of Democracy', is now moving rapidly into the prevailing Latin American pattern of political and social upheavals against a background of physical violence. This trend in Uruguay is incomprehensible to the rest of Latin America, and even to many of the less clear-sighted in Uruguay itself. The appearance in their midst of an armed insurgent movement came as a real surprise to both right and left-wing elements in the country; it was, and is, difficult to explain in the light of Uruguay's long liberal tradition.

But if the rapidly changing events over the past two decades are examined in more detail, it will be seen that the emergence of such a movement was almost inevitable. More surprising, perhaps, is the nature of the confrontation between the revolutionary movement and the older ruling forces. For instance, despite relatively little bloodshed, the movement has become very widespread. A key to the situation may be that ideas have survived from a former period of exceptional political stability and economic prosperity; in such a climate liberal and democratic forms of government became firmly rooted. We should look to Uruguayan history for an interpretation of the present phenomena.

The history of Uruguay as an independent country is something of a paradox. Under their first leader, José Artigas, Uruguay broke away from Spanish rule and moved towards integration and Americanisation. The focal point of Artigas' thinking was that political liberty is impossible without economic freedom; his projects for agrarian reform and the legal protection of native industry and enterprise, together with his unswerving loyalty to the concept of 'the sovereignty of the people', placed him among those who have genuinely fought for independence and self-determination. Unfortunately his ambitions were doomed to remain unrealised because his ideas were ahead of his times.

Ever since the days of the Spanish Conquest Uruguay has inevitably found herself dependent on, ruled by or later influenced by one or other of the great overseas metropolitan powers.

Out of these early beginnings two communities, so to speak, sprang up. On the one hand there was the aristocracy, nurtured by town and trade, and on the other the peasant, the 'Gaucho', to the outside world a romantic, colourful figure, but in reality a member of a depressed sector of the population, subsisting on the periphery of the productive structure, bound to the land and with no guarantee of continued political or even physical existence: material readily available to aspiring rabble rousers or leaders.

The new independent state evolved along well-defined lines. Capital, attracted by the mild climate and rich pastureland on the eastern seaboard ('the cattle ranch by the sea'), enabled the rich to consolidate themselves into a country bourgeoisie. Early this century the decline of local chieftains and the achievement of national unification ensured the capitalistic domination of agriculture and livestock production. Uruguay settled down as a supplier of raw foodstuffs to the rich countries overseas, the cattle-breeding capitalist class retaining for itself a high proportion of the added values on exports.

Democracy was easily and painlessly established at the power-structure level through compromise between the agrarian-exporting sector and the sector which was looking towards an internal market in an initial attempt at industrialisation. No clash was involved as the latter offered no real threat to the basic interests of the cattle producers.

Under José Batlle y Ordonez (1903–1907, 1911–1915) a bonapartist system came to be instituted under which the State acted as re-distributor and set up (by means of a kind of state capitalism) numerous intermediary sectors which gradually turned into the Civil Service and one of the pillars of the Establishment. Meanwhile massive immigration supplied ample labour to the proletariat, that budding prop of local industry. Cattle sold well, there was plenty of money, and a strong consumer middle class imprinted its robust ideology on the country. Uruguay had no class war, no antagonistic factions.

But the world crisis in 1929 threw doubt on the Batllista philosophy. Uruguay's economic drive was generated entirely from abroad and, when conditions in the outside world collapsed, the activities of the agricultural and cattle-producing sectors declined to stagnation point. The carefully balanced conditions essential to Batllism broke down.

The Second World War fostered the development of a substitute industrialisation which loosened Uruguay's dependence on overseas countries. Industry became the dynamic pole of the economy. This situation was further fostered by the Korean War, so the good times lasted until 1955. From then onwards the artificial world conditions, which alone could make such an industrialisation feasible, changed.

The USA had emerged from the War as victor and a dominant world power. In Uruguay the growing national debt was financed by an inflationary process which ate into the living standards of the salaried and wage-earning classes. Unemployment was rife and grew daily worse. The ruling classes began to use State funds as a stopgap. Such manoeuvring capacity as still remained because of the money which had flowed in during the Korean War began to dwindle. All buffers against the enormous economic crises which were gathering momentum were insufficient – and not only insufficient but in fact quite useless. Democracy, that useful political tool in a bonanza era, began to break down.

But whilst the mask could still be kept in place appearances had to be kept up. The great skill of the Uruguayan bourgeoisie has always been applied to smoothing out contradictions rather than polarising them. There has always been great poverty in Uruguay although at times it may not have been very noticeable. The middle class, the most numerous, continued to be satisfied. They had enough to eat, they were being educated, they had a cultural horizon before them. They could accept that a wind of change was blowing everywhere.

But, as deterioration inexorably set in, the more politically aware of the men of this class realised how profound the crisis really was. At the same time the workers were feeling the crunch. They fought for their existence with whatever weapons came to hand, mainly political parties and the unions.

But the ruling powers struck back. Political centres were closed down, newspapers banned, militants imprisoned, demonstrations broken up with gunfire. The legal system tottered and only managed to survive because support was forthcoming for a constitutional reform which, in actual fact, granted the Government dictatorial powers. Uruguay had become a dictatorship in sheep's clothing.

This process did not by any means take everybody by surprise. The traditional Uruguay Left Wing had correctly analysed the crisis. They knew what was happening and what was going to happen, economically, politically and socially, but they failed to draw the correct conclusions and thus failed likewise to adopt the correct political line. Others – from the same analysis – drew different conclusions and their line has been different. They feel, maybe, that force should be countered with force and cunning, and that this countering force is to be found in the people, though they may not be conscious of it. They have to be made conscious, not by preaching to them or spelling it all out. Their consciousness will dawn through direct experience, involvement if you like.

Part 1

Signs of Deterioration

The following fragments are from interviews which I recorded from 1965 to 1970.

Old Age Pensions:
Social Provision or Social Perversion?

When the Eskimos reach an age when they can no longer hunt or fish they wrap themselves in their least costly and warm furs and walk away over the frozen plains; after some hours they lie down on the frozen earth and await death. This custom does not upset anybody. It's just one of those natural things and everybody accepts it.

Here in our sub-tropical paradise on the shores of the Uruguay River we don't have frozen plains where those who become a burden on society can lie down and wait for death to come gently and quickly in the freezing cold. We just have dark, dank basements, damp alleyways, old, broken-down huts, where death comes too, but much less gently. This too is accepted by the rest of the community with a general indifference not unlike that of the Eskimos.

I went down a corridor with peeling walls at the end of which I came to a grey patio surrounded by high, grizzled walls, dark and damp. On the left, where there had once been a kitchen, Julia Merenas had made for herself some sort of a home. She had a bed, a wardrobe, a sewing-machine – very aged – a primus stove, saints, a few photographs, some herbs in a pot or maybe weeds, a tiny splash of green in a grey world. She also had some bottles of medicine, a carved wooden clock and a photograph of some politician wearing a poncho and a white ruff.

'Do you still work as a dressmaker?'

'Yes, miss. I've been a dressmaker for 55 years and more. Do you see this nice blue material? That's left from a special dress I made a little while ago. I've got all kinds of remnants. I've even made a bride's dress once. When Doctor Capurro's daughter got married I made the dress. My name was in the paper. The doctor praised me. I used to have a very big clientele, but of course nowadays . . . well I'm often ill. It's my heart, and the rheumatism.'

'How old are you?'

'Seventy-six . . . Oh, I know I'm not as young as I was. I do get ill often. But as long as I can work I don't mind. I don't believe in giving in to aches and pains. All the same, you can't do so much when you're old. You keep losing things. It's my eyesight, and my hand shakes, and I can't remember things . . . I tell myself that when I really can't work any more I hope God will let me die.'

I went back along the corridor. Some way along a wooden stairway plunged into the entrails of the old slum tenement; it led me to a room inhabited by one Jose Gutierrez. He was standing in the doorway waiting for me.

'Why don't you go inside? You'll freeze out here.'

'I'll freeze inside too, it's just about the same in there.'

How right he was.

He told me about his life. It could all be summed up in one word – WORK. Work, work, endless work. Listening to him you could see how the Biblical prophecy of earning your bread by the sweat of your brow could be taken as a curse. —RIGHT ON!

'I've spent my whole life on the trot. When I was six or seven I was already running errands on the ranches.'

'Did you go to school?'

'Whatever with? Where would the money have come from? At twelve I really started proper work. I can remember one year – 1914 I think it was – I went around numb with cold all the time, dragging hides about for the ranchers.'

'Didn't you sometimes feel you were dying of heat too? In the hot weather?'

'Could be – but I must say I'm so cold today that any sort of heat would be nice.'

'And what do you do now? Do you live by yourself on your 400-peso* old age pension?'

'Live? If only one could. I have a little cart.'

'A horse and cart?'

'I'm the horse,' he laughed, 'an old, broken-down nag. I can hardly drag the cart around any more, only some days when I

* The Uruguayan peso has been enormously devalued in the last few years: In January 1965 the rate of exchange was $1.00 to 22.5 pesos, in November 1966 $1.00 to 88 pesos, in November 1967, $1.00 to 209 pesos, and in November 1971 $1.00 to 600 pesos.

feel a bit better – I seem to choke all the time, you know what I mean?'

'And what do you do with the little cart?'

'When I'm fit enough?'

'Yes, when you're fit enough.'

'I pick up old bones, papers and so on.'

'And you sell them?'

'I sell them. It's a nice little cart. Would you like to see it?'

'OK.'

A few yards along the corridor from his room there was a little two-wheeled cart.

'If I were young, with that little cart – and even without it – I'd cock a snoot at fate – but I'm sick.'

'Couldn't you try to get retirement benefit instead of just the old age pension?'

'Too difficult – you see, I grew up on the cattle ranches – I was always moving from one to the other – and changing my job too. In 1930 I was working on my own as a travelling tinker. When there was a chance I worked with horses; breaking, looking after them generally. I did a bit of shearing too, at times.'

'You broke in horses, did you say?'

'Sometimes – I'd drink.'

'I asked whether you broke in horses – that's a good job.'

'Yes – but a very long time ago. You look at me now and wonder how I could have got down to this. I'm right at the bottom, worn out. I was at death's door twice' – this with a hint of pride in his voice – 'in 1958 I collected sickness benefit.'

'Sickness benefit?'

'Yes, ma'am, I was a lung case. But I only collected for three months. After that I got better and it stopped. Now I'm really sick again. I'm waiting to go and collect my pension to see if they can give me air at the dispensary.'

'Air?'

'So's I can breathe, and pills, for bronchitis, you know.'

'Do you eat well?'

'I'm not actually hungry at the moment – but you begin to get scared when you can't work. You can't live on 400 pesos. If I were young – I wouldn't care. I'd laugh at fate.'

On Calle Alsina, in a room opening straight onto the pavement, a cheerful, dark-skinned woman told me yes, she was on the old age pension, and she was willing to answer my questions. A primus on the floor was all the fire she had, and a cretonne curtain divided her room in two; half was a kitchen, the other half she slept in. She dusted a chair for me to sit on, and sat down herself, obviously pleased to be the centre of attention.

'Ask away.'

'How old are you?'

'Seventy-five.'

'Do you work?'

'Yes – God willing.'

'How long have you worked?'

'Since I was nine.'

'You have a Brazilian accent.'

'I'm from Cerro Largo [a province on the Brazilian border].'

'And what could you do when you were so young?'

'Oh, a lot. I ran errands. I tidied up in the house. I could cook by the time I was sixteen. They paid me five pesos and it was a very good wage, but then the mistress was my godmother. She died around 1920, and everything broke up. I earned less, four pesos.'

'Were you still doing the same work?'

'Yes, I washed, ironed, cooked. I like cooking. But I can't read. If only I'd been able to read. I'd have the recipes read out to me and then I'd do them. I don't think there's anything better than cooking.'

'You look as if you were a good cook.'

'If I weren't so old I wouldn't be stuck here, I'd be around in a kitchen somewhere. I often dream that I'm a cook in a posh hotel, and I pluck fowls until I'm quite tired.'

'Wearing a white cap?'

'Eh?'

'You know, do you dream you are wearing the sort of chef's hat that they wear in big posh kitchens?'

'Do they? I've never noticed. Would you believe it!'

'How long is it since you came here from Cerro Largo?'

'I can't remember. It must have been around 1930 that I was working as a laundress for an hotel here in Montevideo. They paid me four pesos per month. For four pesos I was made to carry the heavy baskets. "Bring the basket," they'd say, "take the basket." It wasn't like it is now, that you charge for every separate piece. You had to lift those great brutes of cauldrons full of wet clothes. I burst one of my lungs, so the doctor told me. And when it rained and the clothes wouldn't dry, I'd have to dry everything with the iron. One day the owner came and yelled at me because the clothes weren't ready. It had rained for a whole week and he wanted me to dry everything by hand with the iron. I picked up the basket and put it out on the pavement. "Find yourself another laundress," I told him. "I'm not coughing up my soul for four pesos." Because I can tell you I used to cough so much I was sure it would fly out of me at any moment.'

'Did you have to pay for the electricity – for ironing?'

'What electricity? Coal, child, coal. They were all coal irons.'

'Do you still work?'

'I can't manage on my pension. Look, I collect the 400 pesos and by the evening I've nothing left. I pay 105 for the rent, 60 for light, about 200 for groceries. I tell you I really get mad. I count up what's left and it wouldn't fill a hole in my tooth. As if I could live without working; as long as I can stand or move I've got to work. When I can't any more . . .' She shrugged.

I recorded six interviews altogether. The people I interviewed were between 75 and 80 years old and they were all sick in one way or another. Of course, given the age of the interviewees, the latter wasn't surprising. What was surprising, however, was that all of them had started to work when young children, and were still working, and all of them, without exception, were absolutely terrified of being unable to work.

I think that if we were to extend this very brief investigation we would find that only the fittest survive to any great age. With such a hard life, many must die long before retirement.

We are all of us Murderers

I first met Pedro when a young woman from VOLPE (a private organisation dedicated to the defence and protection of young delinquents) called me in to defend him. He had stolen a pair of opera glasses because he wanted to go to a football match and see the players close to. His story was very confused. At times he said he had gone into the house to steal and came across the glasses by chance and at other times he said a friend had tipped him off about the glasses and the way of getting into the house. He smiled at me and said: 'If you weren't a toffee-nose I'd tell you the lot and then some.'

'What's a toffee-nose? It must be something pretty bad if you won't trust me or talk to me.'

'Oh no – it's nothing bad – it just means – well, if I say "that fellow's a toffee-nose" I'd mean he was one of those who doesn't know how the other half lives. No offence – but you look a bit innocent and I wouldn't want to open your eyes for you.'

'Shall I show you how wrong you are? You were having a homosexual relationship with the chap whose opera glasses you stole, weren't you?'

'That's right.'

'Why did you steal from him then?'

'Well, he'd promised to pay me a "luca" to go with him, see, and then afterwards . . .'

'Is that a lot of money?'

'Five hundred pesos. But then he tried to rat on me and fob me off with half.'

'What made you think of this method of getting money?'

'Come off it – I was brought up in the orphan asylum and on the streets.'

'Haven't you got any parents?'

'Yes – but I might as well not've had.'

'Any brothers or sisters?'

'I've got a sister of eighteen. They gave her away when she was little. I've tried to see her several times but I don't think the family who've got her want her to know me. They always say she doesn't live there.'

'What was your mother like? Talk to me about your mother.'

'The old woman was plain crazy.'

'Was it she who turned you over to the Welfare people?'

'No – but it came to the same thing.'

'How come?'

'Oh – she'd do anything. One day she got back from work in a hurry – she was going dancing – and me, I was just a little kid then, I'd lost the key to the room. She grabbed hold of me and broke a broomstick over my back. I ran away and went into the police station. She came running in after me. I couldn't get away, I was bleeding all over the place. The sergeant just said "Go on – give him some more" – leastways I think it was a sergeant, I'm not sure, he had stripes on his uniform – anyway he said "They should have laid into you harder." After that every time the old woman went for me she'd say "Go on – go on – go and complain to the cops."'

'How did you come to be taken over by the Children's Welfare?'

'Me – well – I used to wet the bed – see. One day the old woman was in a temper, she poured spirits over me and set light to me. I was two months in hospital. Not from the burns – I'd got over those in a month, but I just didn't want to go home so I kept saying I had a pain all over. For a time I fooled the doctors but in the end they caught on. They had to discharge me, but the old woman had cleared out, they didn't know where to find her, so they put me in the orphan asylum.'

'Was that the Damaso?'

'I wouldn't know – it was just called "the old asylum".'

'How old were you?'

'Seven.'

'Hadn't you been in there before?'

'Yes, when I was one and a half.'

'How long were you there that time?'

'I don't know – two years – maybe more – I don't know.'

'Do you remember anything about that time?'

'I remember somebody – a short woman – who used to beat me up all the time.'

'Why did she beat you? What had you been up to?'

'I don't know – I can't remember.'

'So you had a bad time.'

'Yes – I can remember once being ever so hungry – starving. I ate the paint off my bed.'

'How old would you be then?'

'Four or five. It was around then that the old woman came to see me. She came with a fellow. She brought me some bananas and those round biscuits with sugar on top. She was looking dreadful. The fellow was smashing. He told her they'd better take me away from the asylum. So they came along one day and fetched me. He was a good sort. He worked, doing odd jobs at the race-course. He was OK. Soon after he joined the police and started to bring home more money. He was the cook at the local police precinct.'

'He was cook at the police station?'

'No – no. What I mean is that when he was on night duty at the station he was supposed to see that the constables went out on duty at nine p.m. But if they were playing craps or something and didn't want to move he'd let them stay right through until four or five in the morning, turning a blind eye, then they'd pay him for letting them stay in.'

'So that's what being "cook" means?'

'That's right.'

'Where did you live?'

'We lived near the prisoners' quarters. When he was off duty we used to collect brass oddments, rags and so on, to sell. I used to help him. We didn't do badly at all, we used to eat every day anyway.'

'That was a good time for you.'

'Yeah, but the old woman didn't have the sense to hold on even at this level. One day she had a crazy fit and put me back in the asylum and gave the fellow the push.'

'How long were you in the home this time?'

'Oh – I don't know. I was in and out all the time.'

'Why? Did they get you out again?'

'No – after that I never saw them again. I just used to scarper.'

'Where did you go?'

'Out on the street. I could do well on the street. I'd sell newspapers, shine shoes, sleep in a field or in the market in the banana packing-straw. They used to say there were spiders in it but I never saw any.'

'Were you better off like that than in the home?'

'I'll say. In the asylum you had to do whatever the bigger ones wanted.'

'Such as?'

'The lot.'

'Did you have to sleep with them?'

'Oh – all sorts of things. What they said went.'

'I suppose later on it was your turn to be top dog.'

'Yes – but I'd hardly got there when I heard that as I was fourteen they were going to send me over to Malvin. I got away quickly then, I can tell you.'

'Why – what went on at Malvin?'

'I knew what it was like there, the Principal was mad about nice plump boys.'

'Were you scared?'

'I'll say. He used to get drunk and do no end of damage. I heard recently that he'd been set upon by some kids at the Moulin Rouge and beaten to a pulp.'

'Did that please you?'

'What do *you* think?'

'I think it did. So you were never at Malvin then?'

'Yes, I was. The Flying Squad got me one night and put me away.'

'Was that where you started to have homosexual relations?'

'Oh no – I started on the street.'

'Was that why you ran away from Malvin?'

'That's right, but if you haven't got identification papers you can't hang around the streets for long. The Flying Squad catches up with you and puts you away. Somebody has to stand as sponsor for you and who's going to sponsor anybody for nothing?'

'Weren't you ever fostered out?'

'Yes – a foster mother took me in once. I liked it there. She was all right, but when she found out I had asthma she sent me back.'

'What excuse did she give for sending you back?'

'She told them she couldn't cope with me.'

'Did they believe her?'

'Well, they weren't going to believe *me*, were they?'

'How did you get on at Malvin in the long run?'

'Not bad.'

'What happened to the Principal you told me about.'

'Oh – they got rid of him soon after I went in.'

'Did he retire?'

'Not he – no – the drawers were crammed full of complaints about him, there just wasn't room for any more, so the authorities had to take notice at last. They took him to court.'

'Did he interfere with you?'

'With me? You must be joking. Look at me – I've been this size since I was fifteen, if he'd tried to interfere with me I'd have picked him up and thrown him across the room.'

'Did you have good food there?'

'I'm the boxer type and while I was there I made good use of my weight. Five or six of us used to drink the milk that was meant for everybody.'

'Didn't it matter to you that the other boys wouldn't get anything to eat.'

'Me? I didn't care. I'd learnt at Damaso that you've got to eat to live. I remember one day it was puchero [a kind of meat and vegetable soup]. In those days there used to be an old fellow looking after us at mealtimes. He'd walk up and down between the tables with a little cane in his hands and if anybody tried to talk he'd give them a swipe. Well – on that day I got my plate of mud – soup they called it – and there was a bone in it – no meat. I whistled to the dog and gave it the bone, then I called the old fellow and said "Bring me some food or I'll split your head open." He brought me his own food and didn't have any dinner that day. I was never left to be last when the food was being dished out after that – I can tell you.'

When I saw him Pedro had been in prison for a month. Nobody visited him. 'Would you like me to call somebody so that they can come and see you?' I asked him.

'You could get hold of my old man if you like.'

'I didn't know you had a father.'

'Well – I have. He works in the alpargatas* factory.'

I called his father. 'So he's in trouble again, is he?' he said. I tried to make light of his son's misdeeds. 'OK,' he said, 'I'll see.' But he never did see. During the three months the boy was in jail his only visitors were a Catholic welfare worker and myself. 'Don't you have one single friend, Pedro?' I asked him. 'Yes,' he said, 'I have one, but I don't know where he is, he doesn't have a fixed address.'

When he came out I lost sight of him for a time. One day the welfare worker called me to say he was in Maciel Hospital. He had tried to commit suicide. I went to see him. He was wrapped to the chin in a dark grey blanket. He was thin, pale and his hair had grown so he looked about fifteen. When he saw me he covered his face with his right arm and burst into tears. His other arm was over his chest. His wrists bandaged. After a while he dried his eyes and started to talk about blame and mistakes and forgiveness. The welfare worker who had come along too said, 'There's nothing to forgive. You've repented – God has already forgiven you.'

* Alpargatas are cheap rope-soled cotton or canvas shoes worn by poorer people.

He again covered his face with his arm. 'It's not that. It's that I'm such a coward. I tried to kill myself and I couldn't go through with it, I was afraid. I'm always afraid.'

All this was a year ago. Today we are all deeply concerned because we hear that a boy has been violated and another child excessively beaten. The Press is up in arms and so is the public, and the President of the Child Welfare Council is very upset and makes every possible effort to put everything back into the old channels. With his assiduous help and with a Government Council (Cabinet) which is strongly disposed towards happiness and forgetfulness, we shall all soon be able to sleep quietly in our beds once more. Nevertheless Pedro L. who was not violated by a welfare official, nor beaten until his eardrums burst, is today a lost soul. How can we possibly rest in peace and try to believe that the ten thousand youngsters at present in state care are somehow going to turn out differently from Pedro? What is there to make us believe such a thing?

Penal Institutions:
Idleness as a Prophylactic

In the yard where the prisoners were circulating there was a large placard bearing the words of Article 30 of our Constitution which reads:

'In no case shall prisons be allowed to serve as places where men are mortified; they shall be used only to hold people under process of law or condemned; the aims pursued are re-education, the instilling of work skills, and the prevention of crime.'

Underneath the placard two of the living objects of the proposed rehabilitation – ragged drop-outs – were passing by.

'Are those prisoners as well?'

'Yes, we're short of clothes.'

'Doesn't the prison have a tailor's workshop?'

'Come and see it.'

The workshop was some twenty metres long by six or seven wide and had a zinc roof that was full of holes. In one corner a convict was sewing on a machine.

The remainder of the machines were distributed so as to avoid drips from the roof. The light of a single, low-watt bulb fell on the working convict, leaving everything else in semi-darkness, in the shadows four or five other convicts stood talking and rubbing their hands. The temperature which was down to 5° C outside, could not have been more than 6° C inside. Most of the men were wearing torn rope-shoes known as alpargatas and threadbare suits. They were obviously much colder than I was, and I was cold enough despite my boots, sweater and thick coat.

I was shown a buttonholing machine.

'This machine cost more than a million pesos. It hasn't been used for five years.'

'How do you buttonhole the clothes you make?'

'Clothes? What clothes? It's five or six years since we've seen any underwear. Some of the convicts go into the yard wrapped in a poncho or blanket. Then the warders grumble and say, "Why's he wearing a poncho? I wish I had one." Nowadays they just give the convicts food. Previously they used to give them shoes, because there was a cobbler's shop here. But that's all gone. Now there's just misery and hunger. They don't give out clothes nor do they let the men go into the yard with their own things. They can wear their own clothes in their cell, but not in the yard.'

We went along to the cobbler's shop. It was festooned with cobwebs; the machines – long unused – were rusting away. Three shivering prisoners were pacing around amongst the rusty iron skeletons, moving to keep warm. I spoke to one of them.

'It's not used at all?' I asked.

'No, it would cost too much to put the machines in working order.'

'How long since you've made any shoes?'

'Four years. At first we had no leather, and so it went on.'

'What did *you* do?' I asked one man.

'I used to draw up the estimates.'

'And although there's no work to do – you don't make any shoes any more – you still all come along here?'

'That's right. We have to put in the right number of hours.'

'As for me,' said one inmate who had ten years to go, 'if I had some work to do I wouldn't miss the outside so much. They tell us that the Inspectors, when they come, will fix it so that we have some work. If we get some work again I shall be OK. A man can't be shut up in prison and not do any work, spend his day in the cell. Any book will tell you that. Did you know? It's called . . . called . . .'

'Occupational therapy?'

'That's it, occupational therapy. The prisoner forgets he's unhappy when he works.'

As we crossed a large open yard in the twilight, I saw a sort of shadow up in a high barred window. It was a man looking at us. I knew, I don't know how, that he was waiting for us to go by, under the window to shout something at me. We had just reached the door when his voice rang out: 'Lady, lady, for the sake of your mother listen to me. Don't let them scare you, listen to me, help me.'

'He's a psychopath,' said my guide.

'What's a psychopath doing in here?'

Interview with an ex-convict

Shortly after my visit to the penal colony I interviewed Y.Y. whom I had seen in prison but who had now been released.

Y.Y. is sitting opposite me. He's a man of 50-odd, a fat and placid old lag with a long record in corrective detention and in the penitentiary. He's spent most of his adult life inside, generally for crimes against property.

There is a glass of gin in his hand which he turns gently, smiling as he talks.

'Don't you worry about taking up my time, lady. I've nothing to do until eight o'clock.'

'Do you start work at eight?'

'Me, lady? I never work and I've no intention of starting now. No, at eight I have to stroll along to the prison gates.'

'Are you doing a bit of smuggling?'

'No, no. I go to see my contacts.'

'Your contacts?'

'Yes, I have to keep in touch with my contacts. They bring me business. Mostly they're boys from around here. I've been here so long, as you can imagine, I know everybody around the prison. They know they can trust me. I've known better times, the golden days of prison life when there was plenty to eat and space to move around in and people took you seriously. Now they cram four or five in a cell and the cells only have two beds – when they have any at all. Three of the men have to sleep on the floor. At first they used to make grids to lie on – wooden grids. Now there's no wood left, convicts tend to be destructive, they break things up and burn them. Some of the prisoners don't even have as much as a peso to buy paraffin to heat up water, so they burn whatever is in the cell, see.

'You can't imagine what it used to be like way back in 1937. Do you know there even used to be trunks in which to pack away your clothes? You had the two beds, all complete. It really was something. I can't tell you what went wrong but everything just began to crumble away bit by bit, both in the corrective training part and on the penal side. Degeneration, that's what it is. Years ago they used to line up the men in penitentiary and ask them whether they needed anything, were they short of anything, did they want to have visitors and so on. Treated like human beings they were. They used to give you eight visitor's passes each month so that you didn't have to ask or worry whether anybody would come to see you. You could relax . . . Anyway, you wrote about all this in one of your articles.'

'Oh, you read it did you?'

'Yes.'

'Do you always read *Marcha* [a political weekly]?'

'No, lady. I see it on the stands sometimes but I'm not interested. I only read that number because I knew it would have some of the things I told you when you came round the prison. But you know one thing? You know what you said about mad people? That there are mad people shut away in there?'

'Well, don't you think there are?'

'Oh yes, there are sure enough, but the bad thing is that they aren't mad when they are first shut up. They go mad inside. I know who it was cried out for help from the window. That was W. Wasn't it the window on the second floor just near the entrance, that the shouts came from?'

'Yes.'

'Well, that man – he's one of the "excluded" ones.'

'What do you mean, "excluded"?'

'I mean he's buried alive.'

'What?'

'Buried – that's the word. Listen to me. A man comes into the prison. He's tough, non-cooperative, dangerous they say. Instead of putting him into an ordinary cell and having him seen by a

32

doctor or psychologist or something, they slap him into a special cell. That type of cell is the brain-child of a previous prison governor, a bloke with a twisted, diabolical mind; it'd have to be to have thought up such a place. You can take it from me if you went into one of those cells a bit unstable, you'd come out after 10, 15 or 20 years a raving lunatic.'

'What's the cell like? Tell me exactly.'

'It's solid concrete right through, the bed, the wall, the table, everything. The window has bars and there's a close mesh metal screen as well.'

'How many hours a day does a man have to stay in there?'

'23 out of the 24, 23 solid hours. He's allowed in the yard for just one hour.'

'Who does he talk to?'

'Nobody. I can tell you nobody dares to take these prisoners cigarettes or anything, or to talk to them. If they do they're clapped in solitary for a couple of weeks. At one time the "excluded ones" used to work in their cell. They used to make wire-wool sponges. They were paid 40 pesos per 1,000. But about a year ago they were stopped doing this work. They had to have pliers and wire to work with so the authorities became afraid.'

'Afraid of what?'

'That they might commit suicide – so they say.'

August 1967

Etchepare Colony Mental Hospital: 'That Hell so greatly feared'

I arrived at the Colony towards evening. The men's wards were in separate buildings and these were fairly widely spaced. Through the painted glass of the windows lights were coming on here and there, pale, sickly, bluish glimmers. Save for these and the eerie figures which could be discerned moving between one point of light and the next, the place could have been a ghost town. As we approached I could see that many of the windows were boarded up, like blind eyesockets. The stucco was peeling off the outside walls, showing gashes of raw brick. Through the open doors I could see a dingy interior, grey with the accumulated dirt of years. Outside rats and dogs moved around amongst the inmates, displaying what appeared to be a high degree of peaceful co-existence, though later I discovered this harmony could be shattered.

My first call was to a ward where cases whose mental condition had an infectious disease basis were housed. One tiny 40-watt bulb tried unsuccessfully to illuminate the entrance hall where some 20 to 30 patients were gathered in odd groups. Some sat on upturned boxes or on benches, others crouched on their haunches, resting their bottoms on their heels. Their clothes in rags, their heads bound with more rags in an effort to keep out the cold. On their feet they wore the inevitable frayed alpargatas. Some were heating water in little tins, others cooked what looked and smelt like a nasty greasy pasta. If you saw a theatre curtain raised on such a scene you'd think, 'Ah – drop-outs in a derelict building.'

I moved on into the dormitory. Many inmates were already in bed, most of them had their heads under the clothes. I felt some of the beds: two or, at most, three threadbare cotton blankets. The temperature was 11° C, a mere two degrees above the outside temperature. I commented to the male nurse on the lack of warm bedding.

'You haven't seen anything yet. This is one of the best wards, most of the windows have glass in them.'

I looked at the long row of heads wrapped up in rags, resting on red pillows with no pillow-cases. Among 75 patients I counted five sheets. They were quiet, apparently indifferent to the smell of sewage which violently permeated everything. One inmate called me over and explained at length, in the garbled sentences of a man suffering from a speech impediment, that he had a pain which started in his head and finished in his back. My white trenchcoat made him think I was a doctor. I didn't disillusion him. I pretended to take his pulse and promised him that within an hour he would feel better. Everybody listened to our exchange. I'd hardly finished with him than they all clamoured to tell me about their aches and pains, reaching out their arms for me to take their pulse. I asked what happened if anybody was taken ill at night or became greatly agitated.

'Except in serious cases we manage as best we can.'

'Are you a nurse?'

34

'No, I'm the orderly.'

'How do you manage then?'

'Oh well, you know how it is, one gets used to doing things. In practice all of us orderlies act as nurses.'

As I left I passed an inmate who was tormenting a cat cut off by the flood. I said hullo. He stood up as if moved by a spring.

'Give me a peso to buy maté, please, doctor, kind doctor.'

We collected our sticks and plunged back into the dark. Another ward. The same lack of sheets and pillow-cases. The same dim light, the same shit-coloured walls. The dormitory was however, in this case, well-swept and there was a degree of tidiness. I asked who was responsible for this unusual state of affairs. They pointed out one of the inmates. He was obviously a homosexual. For the first time I thought of the problems that one homosexual among some hundred male inmates would cause, as most of the men were obsessed with sex. I mentioned it to the orderly who shrugged his shoulders.

'We just forget about the whole thing. What can we do?'

I went onto another topic as I'd noticed that most of the windows in this ward had no glass.

'Don't they die of cold? There's no glass in the windows.'

'Well, the last time I saw glass being put in was when the last lot of inspectors came round; that must have been in 1959. They fitted 2,000 panes of glass. They say they're going to replace all the glass again now before they come.'

'Before who comes?'

'The new lot of inspectors.'

'Oh! Yes, I noticed there seems to be a lot of preparation going on.'

'Yes, during the last few days all sorts of stuff has been arriving, blankets, medicines, even doctors.'

'Even doctors? What do you mean?'

'I mean doctors are beginning to come round. They don't usually bother much. Out of 30 on our list only two live in the area. If they live in Montevideo it's not easy to come all this way as often as they should. Besides when they do come they're always in a hurry; it takes them five hours just to come and go – they have the train journey and then the van. And of course this is not their only job They have other places to attend to.'

35

'I suppose the solution would be to pay a good salary and have them full time.'

'Could be.'

We went outside again.

'D'you mind not being able to sleep tonight?'

'Why do you ask?'

'We're just coming to Ward 9. It's the worst ward in the whole Colony.'

'Don't tell me there's worse than I've already seen?'

'Yes. This is it. Most of the inmates are "specifics". They're in the later stages of syphilis. They're not allowed out at all.'

The word 'ward' conjures up visions of sick-care, quiet efficiency, hygiene, peace. None of these could justly apply to any of the buildings I had already seen, but in this case it was even more inappropriate. The place resembled a gloomy, run-down barrack, dark and dirty with a leaky zinc roof. The entrance had double doors, a wooden one and a wire net screen door which was kept closed when the other door was opened. I reached for the bolt and immediately four or five arms were thrust at me through the wire. I couldn't guess whether they were hostile or pleading and my instinctive reaction was to jump back. But I had already learned during the few hours I had spent in this dreadful place that one must always appear calm, sure of oneself, unafraid, so I stood my ground, greeted the owners of the out-thrust hands as naturally as I could and waited for the orderly to open the door.

The first room was the one used as a dining-room. The floorboards were rotten and broken and the earth showed through in patches. In a corner five or six patients huddled around a stove. The expression on their faces was the nearest I had seen to the layman's image of madness. Their eyes were fixed in a hallucinatory stare, their gestures uncoordinated. Despite the stove the cold here was more piercing than in the other wards.

We went out and along to the next ward. It was quite dark by now. My guide bent down fumbling around for something.

'What are you doing?'

'I'm looking for a stick.'

'What for?'

'Dogs. A couple of days ago they nearly killed a woman inmate. Yesterday they seriously mauled another one.'

I hurriedly joined in the search for a stick.

We had to walk two or three hundred yards to reach the next ward. As we approached it appeared to be floating in a cloud of indescribably nauseating stench.

'What on earth is that awful stink?'

'Sewers; blocked sewers and broken pipes. The sanitation of the whole Colony is in a deplorable state.'

As I went up the steps to the ward I discovered that the filthy water was coming from inside and that the whole place – wash-rooms, dormitory, everywhere – was flooded. I wondered how many sane people could have slept a night in such a place without becoming unbalanced.

'We had to take the inmates out of the dormitory and put them in here, the dining-room,' the orderly told me.

'Was that the dormitory? But there aren't any doors. They might as well sleep outside.'

'That's right, but now that the Inspectors are coming they're going to put the doors back.'

A leaky zinc roof is a poor insulator.

'What do they do when it rains?'

'We put the sick ones to bed.'

'And if it rains for days on end?'

'They stay in bed.'

'Are they all "specifics"?'

'Most of them.'

'Do they have a positive Wasserman reaction?'

'All except one. That chap drinking maté with the skinny one.'

'Good heavens, won't he be re-infected?'

'No, the skinny man isn't a syphilis case at all, he's only here for a few days, just by chance.'

'But surely the danger must exist anyway, if not with him, with one of the others.'

'Oh yes, there's always the danger.'

'Why don't you separate them? If they stay in here when they have a negative Wasserman reaction surely it just goes on and on?'

'Oh, they do separate them, but it takes time.'

'I suppose so. Do they at least get adequate treatment?'

'Huh – I order 500 ampoules of broad-spectrum antibiotics and they send me 50. You start treating them, and then you have to stop after a week. It's the same with Penicillin.'

We were in the infirmary alongside the ward. It was no different from the rest. Ruins and filth, filth and ruins. Microbes must have flourished. As we talked we could hear screams and wails. I wrote in my notebook: 'Loud screams – the orderly doesn't seem in the least upset or moved.' I realised suddenly that I myself was not at all afraid and hardly moved. I thought that this must surely be what is known as 'professional hardening'. My overwhelming desire to convey a report that would be as truthful and objective as possible was transforming me into a kind of photographic-machine-cum-tape-recorder. The screams grew louder.

'This ward has the most disturbed cases.' The orderly turned towards the dormitory.

'What's the matter?' he asked the man who was crying.

'They're going to give me an electric shock.'

'Don't take any notice! It's not true. Lie down.'

'Are they very scared of electric shock therapy?'

'What do you think? There was one who used to try to commit suicide whenever he knew they were going to give him a shock.'

'Is it done while they are fully conscious?'

'Of course.'

'I thought you had to anaesthetise the patient before electric shock therapy.'

'That's for the posh sanatoria. Here there's pentathol one day and not the next.'

He went on.

'Look – that's the bed where the taxi-driver murderer slept. They gave him electric shock treatment. They'd plugged him in practically as soon as he arrived.'

'Did he get better?'

'You must be joking – there wasn't anything wrong with him. He was pretending. By now he'll be confessing at Miguelete.'

I said good night and started the long walk to the women's wards. My new guide pointed out the recently mended roadway.

'You see – the whole Colony is getting ready for the coming inspection. It's been announced these two months now, and in two months you can patch up and mend a lot.'

'Time to clear away that mountain of stuff on the riverbank for instance?'

'What are you talking about?'

'You know quite well. Everybody here knows it. There's even

a joke about it, saying that the mountain was swept away by the tide.'

'Well, that's it, you've got it. It was swept away by the river.'

'Except that the "river" has a name and address.'

'If you say so.'

'There are many who say so.'

'Then why do you want me to say it?'

'Because quite apart from increasing the number of reports your evidence is valuable substantiation.'

'Because I am a doctor?'

'Because you are a serious, honest man.'

'Now you're trying to flatter me.'

'In a way. I want you to tell me what happens to the 18,000 litres of petrol which the Colony uses per month?'

'You've said it yourself – the Colony uses it.'

'On one ambulance, one little van which is laid up every other week?'

'There's a tractor.'

'Yes, I was going to ask you about the tractor. Why don't you use it?'

'It's broken down.'

'Why don't you get it mended?'

'Why? Why? Why has all the fruit been allowed to go to waste? Why don't we run an adequate vegetable garden when we have so much land and free labour? Why are there inmates dressed only in a cotton shirt and cotton jacket?'

It was quite late at night when I started a round of the women's wards.

I discovered here that the bed-clothes were generally handed out in accordance with the mental state of the inmates. The more demented, the less blankets. I was hard put to find that any of the really bad cases had more than one blanket. One solitary blanket with a pathetic human form shivering underneath indicated that here was somebody definitely in the last stages of dementia. I don't know why this should have been so but I was able to confirm the fact in the seven different wards I visited. It must somehow be linked to the survival of the fittest.

I discovered too that the work of the female attendant in the colony is about the hardest job any woman in the country can have.

39

She is alone for long hours, shut in with 100 or more mental cases in a harsh and inhospitable building. She has to listen to their screams, defend herself against their furies, pick up the ones who fall out of bed during sleep. All this during an endless night, in utter solitude. The picture is less sinister by day, but equally heart-rending. I have seen inmates messing around in mud and grease and filth, sometimes naked to the waist. The combination of insanity and misery makes a setting which can only be borne by having a psyche of steel.

The theme song of the inmates in the Colony seems to be 'Give me a peso to buy maté'. But here, in the women's wards, another, quite unexpected theme, came up: 'Can you give me a peso for hair dye?'

By now I had run out of pesos, but I said I had a handkerchief I could give the young woman with a bad cold standing guard stiffly at the entrance.

'Don't talk to her, doctor,' cried one of the inmates, 'she's a catatonic.'

I thanked the woman who had given me the information, tucked my handkerchief away and wished, not for the first time, that I had brought a dictionary with me.

It was three o'clock in the afternoon. I had been at the Colony more than a whole day. I had visited wards, workshops, infirmaries, offices; I had talked to doctors, inmates, nurses, orderlies, attendants and administrative officials. I still had the bitterest draught to swallow: the children's ward.

This is a newish building, quite modern, but like the rest of the place, left to fall apart. Roofed with cheerful tiles – which leak. Fitted with central heating – which doesn't work.

There are 76 internees: children of both sexes, with ages ranging from 3 to 14. They are looked after by two girl employees, helped by five or six of the more lucid of the inmates. Some of the children lie in cots, some are wearing strait-jackets knotted behind; they look at me with sad eyes. One should never speak about anybody having 'mad eyes' or a 'mad look'. We don't convey the right meaning when we say that because in fact the eyes of the insane are sad, dreadfully sad.

Several of the children cluster around me, touching me, asking have I brought sweets; am I a doctor; am I going to live there.

Some, I note, look lively and their questions are coherent and sensible. I asked the girl if some of the children were there just for behavioural problems. She confirmed this.

'And is it right that such children should be here? Is this the appropriate treatment?'

I had the answer from one of the Institute doctors some hours later.

'Mentally disturbed children have no place at Etchepare Colony at all, nor should they be anywhere where they can mix with mentally disturbed adults. And there again children with simple problems of behaviour should not live with psychopathic children. And in either case the staff handling them should be specially trained, and the doctor should have constant access to a psychologist for consultations. This would allow for regular testing and recording of progress to see whether treatment was efficacious. Nothing of the sort is done here, and, what's worse, when the mentally sick child attains the age of 15 he or she is transferred automatically to the adult wards, at the most difficult and sensitive age. At the very time when treatment should be consolidated and supervision increased, the youngsters are suddenly thrown in with mental cases of a totally different nature. It's criminal.'

'What about treatment for the adult cases?'

'Treatment here for the adult mentally deranged? The short answer is none. The Colony is just a useful means of shutting them away, isolating them from society. What is really looked for is that such people should not be a nuisance. There's no question of rehabilitation, of trying to make them into useful citizens. There's no such thing as occupational therapy here at all. You could count on the fingers of one hand the inmates who ever leave this place. That's basic.'

'And why is nothing done about it?'

'Do you think that any doctor who has other places as well as this one in his care can possibly attend properly to upwards of 100 patients?'

It was now seven in the evening. The bluish lights were pricking through the painted windows. I could hear the rattle of tin plates. And as for that smell, I'd know it miles away. The stink of the Colony, a mixture of urine, grease and damp. A stench that will remain inexorably and for ever in my memory, lined up with the other collection of smells such as the smell of school, of a wet bus, of a newly-built house.

July 1967

Second visit to Etchepare Mental Colony

Why the fuss? There have always been people who have died of starvation here!

The iron gates were well guarded, and closely bolted and shuttered. 'They've really shut themselves in,' said one of the doctors. 'By now there's nothing left to see anyway, except the macabre setting, and, for those who can get access to the files there'll be a handful of death certificates, all vague: "Cause of death unknown", "Malnutrition", etc., and nobody inside will talk much, you can be sure of that.'

The staff had, in fact, been very surprised at all the fuss outside about conditions in the Colony.

'I don't know what's come over the broadcasting stations,' said one of the attendants, 'such an uproar. There's always been the odd death from starvation here – bound to be.'

'But this wasn't just "an odd death". In July there were 49 deaths compared to 14 during the same period last year. The proportion who actually died of hunger must have been quite high. Do you know how many?'

'No! Honestly I don't.'

'I don't believe you.'

'You'll have to believe me. With the kind of thing that goes on in here death is just something more that happens every day. We couldn't go around asking what somebody had died of. What would be the point? Anyway, the relatives are notified and *they* don't want to know. They leave the poor wretch to us, so we bury him. So why should we worry about why he died? The first I heard about there being anything remarkable about this place was when I heard it on the radio, and that goes for most of the other staff here too.'

While he talked he smoked placidly. Right beside him one of the inmates, stooping double, scraped carefully away at the weeds with a hoe. I bent to look at his face. His eyes were like bits of blue china, flat and lifeless.

'Aren't you scared?' I asked the attendant.

'You people make me laugh. You should have been here twenty-two years, like me and some of the others.'

'I suppose that's how you feel about all those deaths too.'

'That's right. And about all the rest that we don't mention.'

'Such as?'

'Oh, you want to know too much.'

'Do you mean inmates who get out, wander away and get lost and die out in the hills?'

'Them too.'

'What else? Are you trying to tell me there were little children amongst those who died? Is that what you're trying to say?'

'I don't know if there were any died this time.'

'When then? Go on – don't be afraid to tell me, nobody'll know about you.'

'About three years ago, a couple of kids got through the fencing. It wouldn't keep a cat in. They drowned in the bog.'

I went on my way heading for one of the women's wards. When I reached it and went in there was a flurry of activity. One of the inmates was ill, coughing and shivering violently. They'd sent for the duty officer, a nursing practitioner. She looked at the patient. 'What's her temperature?' she asked the nurse. 'We don't know,' said the nurse. 'We can't find a thermometer.'

The duty officer lifted the bedclothes to examine the patient. I turned to the woman in the bed opposite. She was busy hiding some oranges under the covers.

'I see you've had visitors. They brought you oranges.'

'No, the Government sent me the oranges because I'm Red.'*

I set off again and trudged across endless spaces of rough land, thick with weeds which separated the two sections of the Colony. Presently I found myself near one of the kitchens serving a number of wards. On an iron grid about 4 metres by 1 metre, laid over a fire, there were several small pans and one vast cauldron belching forth steam. Standing on the grid one of the inmates was stirring the communal pot with a pole as tall as himself. At times he stirred

* In Uruguay the political groups, of which there are many, are divided into two main Parties, known as Red and White – Red here has no links with Communism and is in fact the ruling Nationalist Coalition Party. The White are the Socialists.

so vigorously that waves of soup and beans slopped over the side. The cook signalled him to slow down and the man obediently stirred more sedately.

Outside in the gathering darkness we could see the inmates, attracted by the smell of cooking, coming towards the kitchen. The odour of the hot soup wafted through the windows, momentarily overcoming the all-pervading stench of urine and old cooking-fat floating like a halo over every building in the colony. They gazed sadly at the kitchen door, vague shapes in threadbare, torn blue cotton garments, their heads wrapped in rags against the cold. They shifted their tin plates aimlessly from one hand to the other.

'Is there going to be enough food to satisfy so much hunger?' I asked an orderly.

'Now there is – there's been enough for the past few days.'

'And before that?'

'Before that there wasn't any.'

'You mean that all those who died of hunger really did die of hunger; literally starved to death?'

'Oh yes. There has been hunger here, there's no denying that. They say that all the fuss they're making now is just politics. To get at somebody and push him down, and raise others. That may well be, but whatever happens or doesn't happen outside, here inside there has been great hunger – starvation.'

'Is it actual lack of food, or is the food nutritionally poor?'

'Both. Food has been scarce since February. First we were short of flour; we couldn't make pasta, which is a staple food, and there were days when there wasn't any bread at all for the patients. It's been a sort of tradition that the sick in here always get three small loaves or baps each daily, but then there wasn't any to be had, and this went on and on. The girls who work in the children's ward used to make a collection to buy bread for the kids. And mind you, those girls earn just a pittance per month.'

'How much flour do you need to be sure of having enough bread and pasta?'

'Sixteen bags daily.'

'How many bags have been coming in since February?'

'I don't know exactly. But I can tell you that often it was much less than half that. Last week we had fifty bags all told, seven for each day, and that was a big improvement, I can tell you.'

'Do you ever get any meat?'

'Very little, hardly any at all.'

'And vegetables.'

'When we see a potato a cheer goes up. The patients have scarcely seen a potato since the beginning of this year.'

'What on earth have they had to eat then?'

'Mainly polenta: a kind of maize mush.'

'What about milk?'

'Yes, they get some milk.'

'So milk and mush is all they get?'

'Milk and mush, mush and milk.'

'And the cold finished them off?'

'Yes, it was often the cold. Certainly in July* more than one a day died from the causes you mention.'

'Isn't that enough?'

'Yes.'

'What medication are the undernourished in here getting now?'

'Caseinate.'

'What's that?'

'A vitamin additive.'

'Have you plenty?'

'It's scarce. But don't think that food is the only problem. It's much more complicated than that. One member of staff for every 70 or 80 inmates isn't enough. And you've got to reckon that in every 80 inmates there'll be easily 15 who are completely unable to do anything for themselves. Have you seen one?'

'From a distance.'

'From a distance? Let's look at one close to.'

'I don't think I need . . . I know just how they are.'

'Come on, come on.'

We went out. We crossed the grass to a ward just like the others. The same stench floating around it. The same perennially wet floor.

'Did you pick this one out for some special reason?'

'No, just because it's the nearest. There are these sort in every ward. Come here.'

He was standing by a bed and I drew closer. He lifted the blanket. Underneath a man was curled in a tight ball; whether he was cold or afraid I couldn't tell. He was no more than 50 years old, I'd say, and he didn't even look at us. 'Aren't you going to eat anything?'

* The coldest month of the year in Uruguay.

45

my guide asked him, holding onto the edge of the blanket. The sick man continued to shiver and did not reply. We repeated this same operation on four or five other similar cases. The result was always the same. Finally he said to me: 'Do you realise why it isn't only a matter of food? How can any of these eat unless they are actually fed?'

I wanted to see the kitchen. But the kitchen was nowhere near the ward; it was some 300 yards away, which presented a further problem as the cauldron, weighing some 80 kilos, had to be carried from the kitchen to the ward daily by the inmates themselves. When it rained, the poor wretches, soaked to the skin and ankle-deep in mud, would drag the great thing along as best they could. Full of soup or stew it would, as often as not, be tepid and well watered down by the hazards of the journey before it reached its destination.

Some days the men just refuse to eat, I was told. They'd rather not. 'I *always* go,' said one inmate who was sweeping alongside us, sweeping more vigorously as he spoke. I approached him and he said, 'I like work – I always work.' He had large, black, wide-awake eyes, lively movements and a kind of wisdom when he spoke; all of which led me to write down what he was saying.

'Everybody here knows I'm better, quite well, but nobody comes to take me away. But I'm quite well. It's just the way it is. My brothers, they got cross with me once and now they don't come to see me. But here I am, working. It's true I earn very little. I get 15 pesos a month which will buy me 10 cigarettes and 100 grams of maté, which isn't much. It's really more a problem of warmth than food. They used to give us nice spaghetti at one time. I suppose they've modernised a bit. They're going to modernise at the Ministry. They say that the Minister is very keen that everybody should have their whack. All the same, if you don't think of the bread being short, things seem to be working out. Sometimes you get the food half raw, and sometimes there aren't any clothes to wear, no trousers for instance. But it isn't like Vilardebo where often you didn't even have any water. I was lucky, they transferred me here. And when it's all modernised it'll be a lot better. They may pay us 30 pesos, or more, and then we'd have our maté and cigarettes. Both at once. I like working. If you don't work you ... you ... Perhaps they'll modernise the place ... My brothers now ... they didn't come to fetch me away, but what's to be done? I'm lucky. I manage somehow, one way or another. Are you very skint? I'm very poor . . . if you had a little peso to spare . . .?'

We made our way back. Along the road the white ambulance was dragging itself along, rumbling noisily and rattling like an old tractor. A few inmates, the last of them, were walking towards their wards. In some windows the bluish lights I remembered from my previous visits were springing up. I was dreadfully tired, as if I had spent whole days tramping around without food or sleep. I had almost forgotten the forty-nine dead who had brought me back here. In their place I could see a multitude of living souls, living lives unworthy of any human being, however mentally cut off, however irrecoverably insane.

One Uruguayan who left*

Many Uruguayans leave the country. You can see long queues of them any morning at the Passport Office. But despite the length of these queues those standing in them are not the majority. The majority leave simply by crossing the river carrying a small suitcase and their identity card. Later, they gradually fetch away the rest of their families, and send for their few belongings.

At first only those whose talents were unwanted and unrewarded in Uruguay left – painters, singers, actors, they all departed. They knew that across the wide river glory would mean more than their names being blazoned in large letters, it would mean a much larger salary cheque.

But that was a long time ago. Soon everybody who had any skill

* During the first half of this century Uruguay was receiving immigrants in fair numbers. During the early 1960s the trend was reversed and people started to emigrate.

In 1960 about 3,156 passports were being issued yearly on an average. In 1961 there were 3,696; in 1962 the number was 6,444; in 1967 9,660; and in 1968 the number had reached a record 17,196.

For the year 1969 the Ministry for Foreign Affairs refused to issue figures. It is common knowledge, however, that so far this year (1970) about 70 people leave weekly for Australia alone. The average age of the people leaving is 29.

According to the census in 1963 the population of Uruguay was 2,600,000, the birthrate 1.3 %.

at all, however humble and unglamorous, left. In Argentina nowadays it is quite usual to find Uruguayans working on newspapers, magazines, as advertising agents, on TV and so on. And the proportion grows daily. Many workers on a humbler level leave, not to make their fortune but to survive at all. The moribund building industry in Uruguay, for instance, feeds the stream of artisans and labourers going across to their more prosperous neighbour. And the more doubtful skills follow in their wake, prostitutes finding rich pickings in their new land.

In Buenos Aires I picked a large construction site at random and asked the foreman whether he had any Uruguayan workers. He said he had two. One was a peasant type who didn't want to talk to me. 'What I think is nobody's business,' was all he would say. The other, a skilled worker seemed less reticent and I was able to interview him.

'Why did you come here to work?'

'If you're going to write down what I say I won't say anything.'

'Why not?'

'We're all applying for our nationalisation papers.'

'What do you mean by all?'

'Me and my brothers.'

'And you think it could hurt you to talk?'

'One never knows.'

'Don't worry, I'll change things so that you can't be identified. Are you married?'

'Yes – I've been married five months.'

'Are you bringing over the whole family?'

'Yes, but not the old people because of their pension.'

'So all the young and able-bodied leave – that's fine for poor old Uruguay, isn't it?'

'Well – what d'you expect me to do about it?'

'What made you decide to come?'

'I wasn't starving or anything, but I'd got some savings together. I've worked for fourteen years – I started when I was fifteen – anyway, I had to keep spending out of my savings recently, so I thought it wasn't good enough.'

'Are you literate?'

'What's that?'

'I mean can you read and write?'

'Oh yes. I went to school and had two years at a tech.'

'What do you do? Have you a special skill?'

'I'm a plumber. Back in Montevideo I had a tiny little business of my own, but when building began to fall off the small people couldn't compete. Materials were so dear. I sold out before I went broke altogether.'

'Have you set up in business here?'

'No – I'm just a worker like everybody else. The money I brought with me wouldn't buy a set of kitchen saucepans. One's got to be patient. I'll make out.'

'What made you first think of coming here?'

'First I thought of going to the USA. There was a lot of talk in the building trade about workers who'd gone to the States and what they earned. But one or two came back and said they wouldn't want to go back. They'd rather be worse off here.'

'Why?'

'Well – you know – they didn't fit in. You earn a lot of money but you know what the English are.'

'The English?'

'Well, they're the same really. They're quite different from us. You can't fit into an English-speaking country. Here, it's like Montevideo.'

'So you decided to come here to Buenos Aires.'

'Not straight off – I thought about it for about six months.'

'Why did you hesitate?'

'Well – er – you know what they say about rats and sinking ships.'

'You feel that Uruguay is sinking?'

'You're a journalist – you must know about that sort of thing more than I do.'

'I'd like to hear what you think.'

'Well – I felt if I hung on I'd just never move at all. I'd get past it.'

'You mean you'd lose the will to get up and go?'

'I was afraid I'd not have the money. You've got to have some savings behind you if you start in a new country. Even if it's not much. Things never work out right away.'

'Are things working out for you, do you think?'

'I get by. I'm not afraid of work – I'll turn my hand to anything.'

'What are you afraid of then?'

'Well – at first I was afraid of the Porteños [Buenos Aireans].'

'Why?'

'I don't really know. Could be because they're aggressive at football. But they're OK now – I think they've changed towards us Uruguayans.'

'What d'you mean?'

'I think they're sorry for us – they think we're down and out. They're always trying to cheer us up.'

'You mean your workmates on the site?'

'Them too – but they aren't really from Buenos Aires, they're provincials. We get Bolivians and Paraguayans on the site too. The place is crawling with Paraguayans. No – I mean the people in the city itself.'

'Let's go back to your life in Montevideo. When did you first begin to feel the pinch?'

'First of all it was clothes. I remember going out to buy shoes and walking up and down the streets and then going home and fishing out an old pair I'd put away three or four years before and cleaning them up and starting all over again with them. Before they'd seemed too shabby to wear, but I was glad to give them another turn. Then there was football. I had to stop going to matches. I like football.'

'What about food?'

'Well, that's when I finally decided I'd have to leave. I found I could only afford spaghetti or corn-meal mush and you get tired of that. Mind you, it wasn't that I wanted to live like a nob or anything, but when everything just drops away suddenly you get frightened.'

'Do you know other workers who've come over?'

'Yes, several.'

'Skilled men like you?'

'All sorts. Labourers, skilled men, all trades. You mention any skill, they've all come. One of these days the layabouts will start coming too. They'll have run out of old newspapers and bits of rag to flog. Even the women are coming.'

'What sort of women?'

'Tarts. Lots of them.'

'How d'you know?'

'Everybody knows.'

'Do they earn much?'

'Any little scrubber can make a packet over here. Charge what she likes – you see it's not allowed here, it's illegal, there's not supposed to be prostitutes here, so there's more demand. The other day on the corner of Leandro Alem and Cordoba I ran into a policeman having a right set-to with one of them. She was screaming at him. "I tell you my permit is up to date." Of course the policeman didn't know what she was on about. I realised she was Uruguayan and when she stopped shouting I tried to explain that in Buenos Aires it's not a question of having a permit. It's against the law to solicit at all. You aren't allowed to walk the streets looking for customers. Later I found she was from Colonia and had crossed for a profitable week-end.'

'How did you find that out?'

'There you go – you bloody journalists want to know too much. I'm not going to tell you.'

'OK. You were telling me that unskilled labourers come over too. How much does a builder's labourer earn here?'

'An unskilled labourer earns 1,700 Argentine pesos per day. But of course being a labourer isn't a trade, you know that, don't you.'

'How much can you buy with 1,700 Argentine pesos?'

'Less than you'd buy in Montevideo for the same money, but back there the labourer would earn half as much as he does here. So in the long run you're better off here.'

'What do you earn?'

'I'm a skilled tradesman, I earn 2,500 pesos per day?'

'2,500 . . . ?'

'Yes. Don't look so surprised. Uruguay's got left behind all right. Well, just think, the death rate is higher than the birthrate over there.'

'And still the young people leave.'

'Well – what d'you expect?'

'What do you miss most about Montevideo?'

'The people mostly. They're happier, jollier, back home. They don't talk as much as people do here.'

'And what things do you think are better here?'

'The newspapers. They're thick and full of news. There's more news about Uruguay here than there is back there. When I write home I tell them what's going on over there. They don't know.'

'You sound surprised – don't you know what's happening back in Uruguay?'

'I suppose it's the Government, isn't it?'

'What else seems better here?'

'Talking of governments, they say this one's not much better than ours back home, but maybe this is a richer country. Anyway, the worker lives better here.'

'Tell me something about your job. Do they do things here the same as in Uruguay?'

'Lord no – they're much more up-to-date here, the way they build blocks of flats and so on. Back in Uruguay you can't go through one flat with the cables and piping and so on to another flat, everything has to go a long, roundabout way. Well here they just do things more efficiently and directly. It's cheaper too.'

'So back in Uruguay because they're old-fashioned and inefficient they have to spend more on materials? Is that what you're telling me?'

'Yes – and on wages. Everything here is much quicker and the people who put up the money get a quick and good return. I've heard it's as much as 50% and the people who buy the flats get them cheaper as well.'

'How long do you intend to stay here?'

'For the rest of my life. I really mean that. What I earn here I'll spend here. I've no intention of doing what some people do, go and live in a foreign country and save money and then go back home to spend it. This is home as far as I'm concerned.'

'Who did you vote for in the last elections in Uruguay?'

'For the late Gestido.'*

'Are you sorry?'

'I don't know. I never thought about it really. How was I to know he'd peg out?'

'If you'd known then that the country would go downhill the way it has, would you still have voted the same way?'

'I'll tell you what. I'll cut my hand off before I ever vote again. I don't want anything to do with the filthy tricks these politicians get up to. I'm a big boy now and I know that all they care about is getting elected. They'll say anything. Then later, when things go wrong they try to cover up. They don't do anything really to improve the country's position. They just spread what little there is thinner and thinner. Just dividing and dividing and dividing so that people get a tinier and tinier bit.'

* Gestido was President from March 1967 until his death in December of the same year.

'You mean devaluing?'

'Same thing. That's all they think of. I shan't ever help them again.'

'Did you always vote for the traditional parties?'

'I always voted for Batllism [at present, Jorge Batlle, great-nephew of the first Batlle who created Uruguay's welfare state].'

'Did you never think of voting socialist or communist?'

'Never – and you know why? Because I think those parties worry about the worker but not about the country, as if the worker and the country were two different things. I think the well-being of the workers depends on the prosperity of the country. They worry about strike pay and that sort of thing, which is all very well in its way, but what about work? Something should be done to prevent people having to strike. And it's no good improving social benefits if we don't have work. Look what's happened to me. A prosperous country has prosperous workers.'

'So you're in favour of development?'

'You're telling me!'

Part II

Now the Poor of America . . .

Now the Poor of America
are really making their voice heard.
History will no longer be able to ignore
them as they are now the ones who are
writing history.

The interviews reported in the following pages were taken between December 1968 and April 1970. They indicate clearly the deterioration in the living standards of the ordinary people, and public disillusionment and cynicism with regard to the Government.

The Men and Women of Tomorrow

Irene is a second-year teacher in one of the many suburban schools around Montevideo. She had been noticing, over a period of four or five years, a drop in the learning abilities of her pupils. One morning, a few months ago, she asked the children, 'What did you have for breakfast this morning? What did you eat before coming to school?'

It was a cold winter's morning but only nine of the children had had a more or less adequate breakfast. Nine out of twenty had had some milk. All the rest had just had a bit of bread, some sweet maté, or nothing at all.

Some months later I dropped in at Irene's school. I had heard about the children going to school on an empty stomach and wanted to make my own inquiries. Not only about what, if anything, children had for breakfast, but about their other meals as well. I wanted to question as large a number of children as possible.

When Irene realised why I was visiting the school she hesitated at first but soon her youthful enthusiasm overcame her scruples and she turned the class over to me.

From her seat I had a fine view through the window, and, in the foreground 20 little heads and Irene's smiling face. I could see that she was a little nervous at the unexpected adventure of a Press interview. I was all set to launch forth on my questions about calories and vitamins when Irene's voice warned me: 'Don't start with the subject you're really interested in – give them time to get used to you, talk about anything.'

Taking the hint I put down my questionnaire and started to talk at random, and gradually, without any guidance from me an image of 'the Uruguayan schoolchild' began to emerge.

In a political context the views of children are not generally given much consideration. As I talked, however, I discovered that here was a completely fresh window through which can be glimpsed the extent and effects of unemployment, the misery and the insecurity which is the lot of vast numbers of Uruguayans. Moreover these children seem to have a very clear understanding of the situation, which surprised me and brought home to me as nothing else perhaps could have done that possibilities for future change lie largely with them.

'Do you like coming to school?' I asked.

They looked at their teacher and then at me and finally at each other until somewhere down the class a small voice piped up. 'Yes.' Immediately a chorus of yeses arose.

'Why do you like coming to school?'

'Because we learn.'

'What do you learn?'

'To read – to write – to draw – to do sums – to work.' A chorus of little voices answered.

'To work? How do you learn to work?'

'I have a friend who sells flowers and he has to do sums to count the money.'

'What's your friend's name?'

'Cacho, he's in third year.'

'So he'd be about eight years old. Can he give the right change?'

'Oh, yes.'

'I work too,' said another voice.

'And me, Miss . . .' 'And me, I work.'

'Now let's see. Hands up all those who have a job.' All their hands went up.

'What? You all have jobs? You, what do you do?'

'I run errands.'

'That's fine. What I really want to know is who does a paid job.'

'I work at the street market. I help a neighbour sell garlic and lettuces and things.'

'How much do you earn?'

'I get 20 pesos and free lettuces – or free other vegetables.'

'What do you do with the money?'

'Oh, I give that and the lettuces to my mum.'

'I earn more than he does.' A little boy next to him was waving frantically.

'Do you? How do you manage that?'

'I go with my godfather to La Paz to buy meat.'

'What – to bring back and sell in Montevideo?'

'Yes – I help him to carry it because the bags weigh 50 kilos and you aren't supposed to go on the bus with heavy parcels, so if there's two of us we can pretend it doesn't weigh much.'

'But it must be quite large – how do you manage?'

'We have to be very sly – we pretend – we smile and talk as if our parcel didn't weigh anything at all, and the bus conductor doesn't realise.'

'And what do you earn for all this?'

'My godfather gives us all free meat. Mum says it's worth more than 500 pesos each trip.'

'Me,' said a tiny mouselike child whose face could only just be seen over the top of his desk, 'me, I draw water and sell it.'

'From the tap at your house?'

'There isn't a tap in my house – it's round the block.'

'And who do you sell the water to?'

'Mrs Cata. She always buys from me.'

'Doesn't she have water in her house?'

'Where I live nobody has water.'

'Who else works?'

'Me!' 'Me!' 'Me, I earn money.'

'OK. What do you do?' I pointed at a little girl who was immediately struck dumb with shyness. 'What's your name?' I asked.

'Margarita.'

'Well, Margarita, what do you do?'

'I clean out the kitchen and Daddy gives me a peso.'

'How old are you?'

'Seven.'

'Don't you have a mummy?'

'Mummy goes to work early.'

'Have you any brothers and sisters?'

'Three.'

'Do they work?'

'No – I'm the eldest.'

'Who gives them their meals?'

'I do.'

'Do you cook?'

'No – I give them what Mummy's left ready in the saucepan.'

'How old is the youngest?'

'Two.'

'What time does your mummy get back?'

'She always comes back at night, except Sundays. She comes back at three on Sundays.'

'Who else works?'

'Me,' said a chubby little girl with round eyes. 'I can use hot water – and I can light the primus.'

'What does your mummy do?'

'She's a cleaner in somebody's house.'

'How many brothers and sisters have you got?'

'Four and me that makes five. Mummy doesn't work on Sundays though.'

'Miss! Miss! I earned ever such a lot of money.'

'Did you now? How much?'

'Thirty-seven pesos. I made a Judas [an effigy for burning at Easter].'

'And what did you do with so much money?'

'I bought some sausages and then I was sick.'

'Miss! I work. I go round with my dad collecting bottles and bits of old iron. We knock on doors and ask if they've got anything.'

'Hasn't your dad got a job?'

'No. He collects bottles and things and sells them.'

I then asked Irene to introduce me to other teachers at the school so that I could carry on with my inquiries. Irene hesitated briefly and then took me along to the fourth year. I was soon talking with the teacher there.

'Yes,' she said, 'the learning capacity of the children has fallen off a lot during the last few years. We find the main causes of slow learning ability are breakdown of family life and malnutrition.'

I asked her about children going out to work. 'There are quite a few in my class,' she said. 'I think seven or eight – would you like to talk to them?'

'Won't I get you into trouble?'

She smiled and ushered me into the classroom.

This was a much bigger class than the previous one. The children's ages ranged from nine to twelve years old. In order to gain their confidence I started to talk about general topics – swimming, football, the cinema. It was an easy step from there to money and from money to working for it.

'Which of you here has a paid job?' Nine hands went up. 'What's your name? How old are you?'

'Maria del Carmen, I'm nine.'

'OK. Tell me about your work – how much you earn – tell me all about it.'

'I look after three children. I work for a lady. She pays me 400 pesos per month. I go at four every day and leave at eight.'

'How do you look after them? What do you have to do?'

'I play with them so that she can get on with her work. I change the baby.'

'I sell flowers,' piped up another voice, 'jasmin, or violets when they're in season.'

'How much do you earn?'

'It's always different. The more I sell the more I earn.'

'Miss! Miss! When it rains he doesn't earn anything.'

'It rained yesterday and I earned some money – so there!'

'What does your father do?'

'He mends blinds. Goes round the houses mending those blinds that roll up. He hasn't had a job for seven months.'

'What did he do when he was in a job?'

'He's in building.'

'Miss! He works in a chemists shop.' A small fair-haired boy pointed to another boy sitting at the back of the class. 'He earns more than anybody. He earns 1400 pesos.'

'Is your father out of work too?' I asked the budding plutocrat.

'I don't have a father. I live with Mum and her man. He's a policeman.'

'If he's a policeman he must have plenty to do?'

'Yes,' chorused the whole class.

'And why are policemen so busy?'

'They have to keep an eye on the banks – and there's so many laws – and the students, they make a lot of trouble.'

'How do they do that?'

'They throw stones – build barricades.'

'Do you think they're wrong to do those things?'

'They do it because of their friends being killed, and to get silly laws changed, and so that working people can earn more money.'

'The students are on the side of the workers then?'

'Yes. My dad's a worker and my brother's a student. But my dad doesn't want my brother to get mixed up in these things. He says he's too young.'

'Doesn't your dad want the students to help the workers?'

'Course he does – but he says it's dangerous and my brother's only fourteen.'

'So your brother doesn't go along – doesn't demonstrate?'

'Yes, he does – he goes just the same.'

'So he's brave – and disobedient.'

'Yes, he told my dad he was the toughest in the class.'

'I have a cousin who's a student,' said another voice.

'That's good. Why else do the students fight?'

'Because some people don't have enough to eat or anything and other people have too much money. They have big estates and they go to the casinos and play roulette and they go and stay at the beach at Punta del Este and some people can't afford to pay a short bus fare.'

'Have any of you ever been to Punta del Este?'

'I have.'

'Tell me about it.'

'I don't know – there were a lot of trees.'

'Miss!' said another voice. 'I know what it's like – it's like a millionaire's bar.'

'Is it? Who told you?'

'I saw it on telly.'

'We have a telly too,' said another voice.

'What programmes do you watch?'

'Gunfights – war.'

'Is there a war going on anywhere in the world right now?'

'Yes – in Vietnam.'

'Tell me what you know about Vietnam.'

'They're at war against the USA.'

'And why are they at war against the USA.'

'Because the USA wants to grab all their riches.'

'What riches?'

'Their land – livestock – oilfields.'

'And why should the USA want those things? Is it a poor country?'

'No – they're rich – but they want more.'

'Why should they want oil?'

'To make petrol and paraffin.'

'What for?'

'For their cooking stoves.'

'Are they short of paraffin for their cooking stoves in the USA?'

'No – they have electric cookers.'

'Why do they want petrol?'

'For their tanks.'

'Why do you think the USA wants tanks?'

'So that they can grab other countries.' — *very good, right on!*

'Is there any oil in South America?'

'Yes – in Venezuela. A lot.'

'So in Venezuela everybody must be rich.'

'No – because the USA takes it.'

'What else does America take from South America?'

'Chile's copper.'

'What do they take from Uruguay?'

'We don't have much.'

'So we are a poor country?'

'Well – we're in debt – in pawn.'

'What does being "in pawn" mean? Who knows about pawning things?'

'To pawn things you go to the pawnshop.'

'What's a pawnshop?'

'A place where you take things like rings and radios and transistors and they lend you money.'

'And what does a country pawn?'

'Its land – its production – its livestock.'

'You say our country is in pawn – who is the pawnbroker?'

'The USA – and other countries too.'

'Miss!' called out one child, 'in the old days the gipsies pledged their lands and now they have to go around living in little tents wherever they can.'

'So you think that any day now we Uruguayans are going to have to start going about living in little tents?'

'No, because we shan't pawn anything more.'

'That's what you say, but you don't give the orders. If the Government wants to pawn things they'll pawn whatever they want,' said another child.

'So it's the Government's fault? They put us in pawn? We don't do anything? We just sit around?'

'We have to wait for the next election,' said one child. 'We could have a revolution,' said another.

'A revolution? Who would revolt?'

'The people.'

'What? Just like that? Do we all get together and . . .'

'No – you've got to find somebody to lead you.'

'How would one go about finding a leader?'

'I don't think there's anybody just now,' said one child. 'If only Artigas* was alive today,' said another.

'Was Artigas a good leader? And are you sure he would have wanted to lead an uprising?'

'Yes – because he wanted everybody to be equal.'

'And aren't we all equal now?'

'No – because the Government is on the side of privilege.'

'What's privilege?'

'You give more to those who have a lot and you don't give anything to those who haven't got anything at all.' *JUST like Ame*

'You mean they don't give anything to the poor?'

'Yes, they do – they give them beatings.'

The teacher smiled. 'Don't think we teach them these things. The children you've heard are not the more studious or thoughtful ones. Mostly they're the ones who mature early because of the sort of life they lead. This is a working-class district and the children come up against these problems daily in their lives. We try to encourage them to reflect. We believe in the old precept "The child should think and inquire".'

I had no difficulty about getting into the next class. The teacher there had clearly not understood whether I was an inspector, an assistant teacher or a foreigner going around visiting schools. I didn't make any effort to explain myself to her. She gave up her seat to me and collaborated willingly.

'Hands up those children who have a paid job.' (Eight hands shot up.) 'Each of you who works must tell me how much he or she earns, how many hours are worked and where this work is done.'

'Miss! I work in a mat factory. I work seven hours and earn 5,000 pesos.'

'He's a tycoon,' said a dark-skinned little fellow in the front row.

* José Artigas, the Liberator, hero of the Independence of Uruguay.

'Do you work?' I asked him.

'Yes. I go with my dad to market three times each week.'

'Don't we know it,' said the teacher, 'he sleeps all though class afterwards.'

'I help my dad make brushes – I don't earn anything – I help him because he's out of work.'

'Me, Miss!' said a small girl. 'Me – I work with a dressmaker from two till seven every day and I earn 1500 pesos. My sister's sixteen and she earns 2000 each fortnight but she has to work twelve hours a day.'

'Twelve hours? Can't she change her job?'

'Oh no, Miss! She's looked and looked for another job but there aren't any. If she left her job somebody else would take it right away and then she wouldn't have one at all.'

'Are jobs scarce?'

'Yes – very.'

'Why do you think that is?'

'Because there're all sorts of things that aren't used.'

'Such as?'

'Well – manganese.'

'I didn't know about that. What else?'

'The land.'

'What happens to the land?'

'It's held by the rich landowners and concessionaries.'

'Why do they hold it, do you think?'

'For themselves. And it's not properly used. It doesn't produce enough.'

'What do you think one could do about it?'

'They could be asked to help the poorer people by giving them a part of the land.'

'Do you think that would be easy? Would the landlords agree?'

'No, Miss – they wouldn't agree. You've got to have agrarian reform.'

'What's that?'

'You share out the land to everybody—' 'You divide it up—' 'Everybody has their own bit to cultivate—' Several of the children spoke at once.

'It sounds a good idea – why isn't it done?'

'Because it wouldn't suit the landlords.'

'And would it be good for the country?'

'Yes – but the Government doesn't want it either.'

'Why not?'

'Because the Government is rich.'

'The Government?'

'Those who govern – they are the landlords and their friends.'

'So what can be done?'

'The Government must be changed. We'll have to vote again.'

'That means waiting a long time, doesn't it?'

'You could talk to the Government,' said one child. 'But they wouldn't listen,' said another.

'How do you know they won't listen?'

'The Government doesn't want anybody to stand up against them. They like to be listened to but they won't listen.'

'How do you know all this?'

'Well – when the papers say something against the police the bits are blanked out. The paper is published with blank places in it.'

'Doesn't the Government know what the police do?'

'Oh yes, but they don't want the newspapers to go around talking about it.'

'What newspaper had blank bits in it?'

'The *Extra* and the *Popular*.'*

'Any others?'

'No.'

'Does anybody here read *Marcha*?' One hand went up.

'My uncle buys it – it's just a tiny paper.'

'So you all think the Government should listen to you but won't. How do you know they don't want to listen?'

'Because if anybody goes out on the street and speaks out or anything, they're locked up straight away.'

'Who goes on the street to speak out?'

'The students and the workers – but mostly the students.'

'Why do they protest?'

'Because they're brave.'

'They're certainly brave, but what are they trying to do by protesting?'

'They want prices brought down – and they make demands for the workers too – and ask for materials for the technical schools.'

---

* The *Extra* is a newspaper of the independent Left, the *Popular* a Communist newspaper.

'Miss! The students once grabbed a policeman and he had an extra gun on him as well as the regulation one.'

'What did they do to him?'

'I don't know; my sister told me about it. But they got hold of him because the police were going around saying the students were making bombs and things and it wasn't true.'

'If the students weren't armed what did they fight with?'

'They had catapults, and the police, they had bullets as big as this.'

'Good heavens, if they were that big they'd be cannon balls.'

'Well – maybe a bit smaller.'

'You've all been telling me that the Government won't listen to the newspapers, nor the students – that they don't want to listen at all. It's awfully hard to make somebody listen who doesn't want to. What could we do?'

'We could write letters to them, Miss. A lady next door to me once wrote a letter to the Legislative Palace.'

'Did she get an answer?'

'I don't know – I don't think so.'

'Miss, somebody could be kidnapped – like Pereyra Reverbel.'*

'What?'

'Yes – like the Tupas did with Pereyra Reverbel.'

'What are the "Tupas"?'

'Tupamaros.'

'Yes, I know – but who are they?'

'Oh – they're a big band of people who want equality and justice for everybody.'

'Are they a political party?'

'No.'

'Why don't they form themselves into a political party?'

'Because if they did they'd have their meeting places and clubs and things – where they have meetings and give speeches and so on – they'd have them all closed down and the Government would arrest them all.'

'Why would they arrest them?'

'Because they want to help the poor and this wouldn't suit the Government so they say the Tupamaros are bad – wicked people.'

'Well, they do hold up banks and so on, don't they?'

* See the Postcript.

'Miss! Miss! That's not true. They don't hold up banks. The police say it so that they can arrest them and take them away.'

'Have they taken them all?'

'No – they're all over America.'

'Who told you they're all over America?'

'My sister told me. She works in an office. She told me that they have them in every country but they have different names, that's all.'

'I see. But going back to Pereyra Reverbel – why do you think they kidnapped him?'

'So that they could tell him everything. He'd have to listen, you see. And then when they let him go he'd go back and tell the others in the Government.'

'I don't think that's a very good way of making the Government listen. Do you think it's easy to kidnap somebody?'

'Oh no – you've got to be really smart to be able to do it. A real top-notcher.'

'So it's difficult. What else could be done to make the Government listen?'

'Miss! I . . . I . . .'

'What's your name?'

'Laura.'

'OK, Laura – what's your solution?'

'Well – I think the whole Government should come and spend a month – or maybe just a few days – living the way we do. The way we all do.'

'And how do you all live – how do most people live?'

'Well – we could make them come and live in a tenement or shanty town, and they wouldn't have any work and no money and couldn't move somewhere else or take a bus to go and look for work.'

'What else? Come along now – somebody else suggest something.'

'They could have dreadful toothache and there'd be no dentist or hospital for them to go to.'

'What else?'

'They'd have to give away their pet dog because their parents couldn't afford for them to keep it – even if they loved it ever so much.'

'What else?'

68

'They'd have no television – and not even a tiny, cheap, little Christmas tree.'

Amen.

The Meat Workers' Strike: 'Just as God would have wished'

Even a quick survey of the long strike by the workers in the meat industry* would seem to show new aspects and patterns, which mark this particular strike as different from others. On this assignment I interviewed – at random – workers, their wives and their children.

B C, 38 years old, meat worker
'Do you think there are features about this strike which makes it different from other strikes?'

'For us workers at the Frigorifico Artigas there never were any strikes, so this one can't be different, can it? We had a union – some union – it was laughable. We had no solidarity with anybody. I don't know how the union leaders were chosen but they always backed the bosses – just think – union headquarters was set up inside the establishment. We hadn't had a strike for 10 years.'

'Well – you've had a beauty this time to make up for the 10 years.'

'Yes – first-rate.'

---

* The meat industry is of tremendous importance to Uruguay and the strike caused serious disruption.

The huge 'frigorificos', as the meat-packing plants are called, are really like whole towns – self-contained communities, with a vast complex of factory buildings for processing the cattle and for the production of by-products, canned goods, etc. Many of them have their own housing estate, a hospital, shops, churches, schools, etc. Very often the plant gives its name to the district, and the whole life in the area is bound up with the plant, particularly as it is often the sole employer with the livelihood and welfare of thousands of men and their families in its power.

Many of these meat plants – famous household names – were established by powerful international organisations such as Swift, Armour, Anglo (Vestey), etc. The plants mentioned in the following interviews – Frigonal (Frigorifico Nacional), El Cerro, Frigorifico Castro, Fray Bentos – are amongst the largest and most important in Uruguay. The industry as a whole is going through a great many changes at present.

'What – if anything – have you learnt from this strike?'

'In the first place we've now a good idea of the value of being united.'

'You mean unity of all the workers taking part in the strike?'

'No – that goes without saying or there'd be no strike.'

'I don't understand.'

'I'm talking about the people from the other plants, Cerro and Castro, who've never set eyes on us, but who were behind us. And the ordinary people too. Before, when the men went out on strike and you had to try to raise funds by selling flags and so on, you could see people thinking "why don't you go to work instead of begging". But this time all of us who went to sell flags to raise funds, or do other jobs, we could feel the people were behind us.'

'So that's what you call unity.'

'Yes, this solidarity – unity – whatever – was the biggest thing behind this strike. When the Union knows it has the public behind it, it knows it's really gained something.'

A C, 40 years old, woman worker

'What did you think of this strike?'

'Oh – this was a real, proper strike, just as God would have liked it.'

'Does God have anything to do with strikes?'

'In some strikes the devil does – but not in this one.'

'How could you see the devil wasn't in it?'

'In the way everything was organised, how the camps functioned. Anybody who was short of food knew they could go along and get food for themselves and their children.'

'How did this all come about?'

'Because we had the backing of the public in general, and the students especially.'

'Did the students help financially?'

'Not only did they help financially, they attended our meetings and discussed our problems with us.'

'This thing about student/worker collaboration has ceased to be just a May Day phrase, then?'

'It may not be the first time they've helped, but it's the first time we've been helped this way. They seemed to be the same as us, and when we had to face the police or build barricades, they were in front.'

'Don't you think in that sense there was an important difference between this strike and previous strikes?'

'In what sense?'

'There being violence.'

'Maybe. There have been other violent strikes. Still, there's something which might have been different.'

'Yes?'

'I think this time we knew where we were going.'

'How do you mean?'

'I mean – oh, I don't know – there were times when one felt the whole of the Cerro plant would go up in flames. The people weren't afraid. There was no fear at all. You've no idea how many kids of twelve or thirteen we had to drag out from under the horses' hooves.'

RZ, 10-year-old son of a worker at Frigonala

He was selling flags at the Pantanoso bridge.

'Tell me, what do you know of the strike?'

'I don't know anything. I just sell flags to raise money.'

'Do you like selling flags?'

'Yes.'

'So you sell them to amuse yourself?'

'No – I sell them because everybody has to help. If they don't the strike will fail.'

'And if everybody helps?'

'If everybody helps, the strike succeeds.'

'Is it always like that?'

'Yes.'

'What other things can one do to help, besides selling flags?'

'Do you want to help?'

'Me? All right.'

'Then you can buy some flags.'

In the doorway of the Hurricane Club the workers from the Frigorifico Rio Negro were sitting under a thin winter sun, drinking maté. It was nearly a month since they had arrived with their wives and children after a march of several days. I interviewed them as a group. I asked them what events had struck them as important in bringing about the final victory.

'The most important was having complete solidarity. It's years since the Artigas plant went on strike, and the up-country packers, although they are relatively newly established, stood firm. The support of the other unions was also important. It's not the first time we've marched like this, but other times the people who met us on the way could be counted on the fingers of one hand. This year whole unions turned out to support us; and the student movement.'

'Could you have discussions, dialogues?'

'A priest came to talk to us about the new structures that have to be built up in Latin America if we are to develop. And everybody helped us during the march, one way and another.'

'Tell me more about the priest.'

'He wasn't the only one who came during the march. A lot of them came. And one said that at this stage we had to know that with some people you can't have a dialogue because "there can be no dialogue between the hungry and those who starve them, nor between oppressed and oppressor".'

'Are you in agreement with that? Do you believe that dialogue is already useless?'

'I think it does little, if any, good.'

'Besides,' said another man, 'those who talk are taken away.'

'I don't understand.'

'What I mean is that the most intelligent and articulate are the first to be put in prison.'

'Which means?'

'Which means that it is better to talk less and do more, so that when they wipe you out, at least you have been wiped out for something worthwhile.'

'What do you mean by "do more"? What does "doing" mean as regards yourselves specifically?'

'One changes as one goes along, it used to be that we'd think one thing worth doing; today it's something else; tomorrow it'll probably be something else again.'

'Today it's marching?'

'Marches, barricades and stones.' He smiled.

'Why do you smile?'

'I don't know – I'm a bit sceptical about what can be said in the heat of the strike. Later on when the elections come round, they still believe everything they say.'

'Is it a long time since you believed in the Three Wise Men?'

'Quite a long time. However much honey they pour into our ears we know what's what, and that they govern for the few.'

'All this that you're all telling me, what does it mean in concrete terms?'

'Which of the things we say? Maybe what you want to know is what we are going to do at election time?'

'Yes, that'll do.'

'We'll cast blank votes. Those who get returned to government will get there with a thin scraping of support.'

'My first question was . . .'

'. . . whether we'd learned anything from this strike,' one of them finished for me. 'Yes, we've been confirmed in an idea we already had: that all the time more and more of us are coming to know that you can't believe a word of what these men say who get up on a rostrum a few days before the elections and talk about full employment and schools and hospitals. More and more of us have stopped believing that parliament can solve any problems. We know now that arms have to be met with arms.'

E L, 35 years old, worker and union leader

'What's important and new about this strike?'

'In the first place we had total solidarity and unity. When I say total I include the unions up-country who have for the first time come massively into line with the main union. Another new feature was the camps; these were not only new but in one sense they were very important.'

'Workers could be happy that their children were not depending on their wages to be able to eat? Is that what you mean?'

'Yes, but equally important was the permanent contact between the men in the camps. This did away with the "week-end strikers" – those who stayed at home and watched it on TV and went to a meeting once a fortnight. Now all the workers were really up to date with what was going on. The lies in the Press and on the radio could have no effect. Everybody knew immediately about the problems. They discussed them, proposed solutions. There came a moment when we realised that if the whole leadership of the union was arrested, there was already sufficient human material qualified and capable of replacing them.'

'How did you get round the Government Decree prohibiting strikes?'

'Up-country they didn't get round it; the camps were broken up. Here they only broke up the Castro camp. The mounted police rode in and broke up everything – tables, cooking stoves, flags, loudspeakers – the lot.'

'Did they tear up the flag?'

'Tore it up or burnt it. I can't remember which. The men exhibited what was left of it afterwards with a placard explaining what had happened to it.'

'What happened at Cerro's camp, are they still OK?'

'It wasn't easy to get into Cerro's camp. They'd have to take it with gunfire, the public was completely and solidly behind the strikers.'

'Was this solidarity backed by contributions of hard cash?'

'Not only by hard cash. When the police went in to break up the Castro union's camp the housewives in the district helped the workers by pouring detergent on the roads to make the horses slip.'

'What about the church? Did the churches at Cerro collaborate in any way with the strikers?'

'Yes – completely. There are four churches in the Cerro complex and they were solid with us. Sometimes we used the churches themselves as a refuge and whenever there was a big demonstration the priests let the schools out. The most recent occasion was on 14 August, the anniversary of Liber Arce.'*

'How do you evaluate the help of the unions affiliated to the Trades Union Congress?'

'Most important – absolutely vital. We received enormous amounts of money and quantities of foodstuffs.'

'Do you think that this experience which the workers have lived through will have weakened the faith that many of these men used to have in the various traditional political parties?'

'Yes – it was an eye-opener to see the local politicians who operated within the traditional political set-up hurriedly taking down off their front doors the cards showing the political clubs or groups they sponsored.'

RB, 10 years old, daughter of two workers at Fray Bentos
'Is it true that you walked all the way from Fray Bentos?'

'Why do you look at my feet?'

---

* Liber Arce was one of three students killed by the Montevideo police during a demonstration in August 1968.

'I'm just thinking what a long way those little feet have come.'

'My feet aren't that small – I take a size 32 shoe.'

'Anyway, Fray Bentos is a long way away.'

'Yes – but I didn't have to walk all the way. I wanted to but they wouldn't let me. Sometimes they'd let me, then I'd walk, but mostly I came on the bus.'

'How many of you came by bus?'

'All those under fourteen.'

'Tell me all about the march – right back to before it started off from Fray Bentos.'

'Shall I tell you right from when we went to the Plaza?'

'Yes, please.'

'We all went to Plaza Artigas – and there Macedo gave a speech.'

'What did he say?'

'He said we had to fight to the end – I don't remember every-thing he said. Then a priest spoke. He said we all had to be as one, and he said the most important thing was that the mothers on the march must look after us.'

'The children? And what else?'

'Yes, they had to look after us children. What else? Wait a bit – he said "Unity is strength". Then Macedo went with us to the boundaries of the estate and there a lady got up on a box and spoke. She said we mustn't cry.'

'Was somebody crying?'

'My mummy cried for a while.'

'Why did she cry?'

'She was thinking how dangerous it was. My brother cried too.'

'Was he thinking of the dangers too?'

'No – he didn't care about danger. He cried because he'd been taken ill and had to stop behind when he was enlisted in the march and everything.'

'But if he was left behind at home how did you know he cried?'

'Because my other brother told him if he didn't stop crying he'd be much worse. And he was very ill.'

'So you started off from the boundaries of the plant. Tell me what happened then. What did you like most about the march?'

'I liked everything except sleeping on the ground. I had to sleep on the ground because our bed was too narrow and only fitted

Mummy and my young brother. What I liked best was arriving at Mercedes because they gave us no end of presents, donations and so on. They gave me these shoes. They brought us books too, and biscuits, and a boy came to sing and entertain us.'

'What did you have to eat on the march?'

'Everything – we had vegetable soup, chocolate, bread and jam, rice, coffee and milk.'

'Did you eat a lot?'

'Yes – some of us got fat because wherever we went they gave us things.'

'So the only thing you didn't like was having to sleep on the ground?'

'Yes – that – and when we all had to turn back.'

'When was that?'

'At Kilometre 139. The police wouldn't let us go on.'

'Did you see them?'

'No – it was night time and us children weren't allowed to go where the police were.'

'If they wouldn't let you through how did you get here?'

'Because somebody sent two lorries – I don't know who it was, somebody – to take the children and the mothers. They put us in there with the bags and the mattresses and tents and covered us up with a tarpaulin so that we wouldn't be seen.'

'Were you frightened?'

'Yes – I was for a bit. Then Mummy said one mustn't be afraid of the police as it only makes things worse. And then I fell asleep.'

What do the Tupamaros mean to you?

This series of thumbnail interviews was recorded in an up-country area familiar to the writer who had discovered that the National Liberation Movement was almost completely unknown up there. This lightning survey was carried out to discover whether the movement was now better known after their exploit at San Rafael in February 1969, when they raided a big hotel near the seaside resort.

The interviews were all recorded in the countryside around the town of Maldonado.

A D, 45 years old, dairy farmer – primary schooling

'What do the Tupamaros mean to you?'

'I couldn't say. I'd say they're a bad lot, but I don't know what they're supposed to be trying to do. They're said to be Communists. But I wouldn't brand them as either bad people or Communists. I saw when Monty's* was held up. Who were the real villains, I'd like to know? Those who went in with a machine-gun or those inside lining their pockets? The Tupamaros don't frighten me. What's more if they *are* Communists that doesn't scare me either. You know what *does* scare me? Those people who go and play roulette and gamble three or four million. If I knew what the aims of these Tupamaros were maybe I'd even help them. It's not that I'm . . . No – I'm not anything. Don't you go thinking things. A while ago some chap was up here to measure my land.'

'What was he – a land surveyor?'

'That's right – an educated man anyway. He told me, "I think those people are doing something worth while – I'm not really sure – but if their cause is a good one . . ."'

'Do you belong to a political party?'

'I was always a "White".'†

'White?'

'Hold on, though. I was a White in the time of Herrera. Since the old man died it doesn't sound so good to say you're white.'

C F, 37 years old, labourer working on the highway – primary school to 4th year

'What do the Tupamaros mean to you?'

'I'd have to ask *you* that. You tell me – what are the Tupamaros?'

'You mean to say you've no idea what they are?'

'Now look here – I live over there, in that hut you can see. I've five children and another on the way. The hut leaks like a sieve. What time would I have to think? I'm a labourer and labourers aren't much given to thinking.'

'What about newspapers? Don't you read a newspaper?'

'What papers are going to get out here?'

---

* Financiera Monty – a big financial firm.
† The political parties in Uruguay are divided into Whites, which are the various Socialist groups, and the Reds, which are the Nationalists – inclined to conservatism. The ruling power at this time was a coalition of the Nationalists under Pacheco.

'What about the radio?'

'The radio? When I've enough money to buy the batteries, which get dearer and dearer. Besides . . .'

'What?'

'I don't like what you say about working for a newspaper.'

'Don't worry about that.'

'I don't believe what the papers or the radio say – not much anyway. Those people you ask about. Some people say their intentions are good. But you can't photograph intentions.'

'Don't you like them then?'

'Frankly no. But they don't bother me.'

R B, 32 years old, tractor driver –
primary school to 4th year

'What do the Tupamaros mean to you?'

'Who are they? I've never come across any?'

'You may have, without knowing it.'

'Oh – well, that may be.'

'Suppose I were a foreigner and I asked you to explain to me what they are, what their aims are, what they aspire to do. What would you tell me?'

'I'd tell you they're against the Government and want to improve the lot of the workers.'

'How do you know they want to improve the lot of the workers?'

'Because they said so at Punta del Este.'

'What did they say?'

'That they were doing it all for us, for the workers.'

'They could just have been saying that.'

'No – because afterwards they returned the money to the employees. Have you ever known a thief return money?'

'No – But what you're saying about the money being returned wasn't like that at all. They wanted to return the money but it wasn't accepted because there were conditions attached to returning it.'

'There you are. What did I tell you. They take everything.'

'Who are "they"?'

'Those on top. They're eaten up with pride and the worker can go hang. Excuse me if I don't say any more. If this were Montevideo – but here one just listens to the radio, there's nothing else to go by.'

'Do you always listen to the radio?'

'Yes – although one knows very well that they just tell you lies.'

C C, 27 years old, labourer working on the highway –
3 years primary school

'I'll answer your questions for you to write it in your paper, but first you've got to put in what I'm going to tell you.'

'Go ahead.'

'You've got to say that we got an increase of 7%, which is just mocking the workers.'

'How much do you earn per month?'

'When the weather is good – very good – I make 12,000.'

'12,000? How many children have you?'

'I've got three – but hold on – I don't draw the full 12,000. They take away 12%. I never make even as much as 10,000, and when the weather's bad I don't even get half that.'

'OK. I'll put all that in. Now about what I was asking you.'

'Truly – I don't know. I can't give an opinion. Those are very odd ideas, aren't they? I've never thought about it really. What do you think?'

'Me? Nothing. I think you have a good idea of what it's all about but you don't dare to speak.'

'You think I'm scared?'

'Maybe a little – aren't you? Let's see, would you say they are delinquents? Criminals?'

'Oh no!'

'Why not? They do things criminals do.'

'Yes . . . er . . . no.'

'Well, we are getting somewhere. Although they sometimes carry out hold-ups or robberies you say they aren't criminals. You must have a reason for saying they aren't. Now think.'

'Well – they don't behave like common robbers. They tried to give the money back to the employees in the Casino. And they always act more or less the same way – they have a sort of pattern. Besides that lad from San Carlos who is in prison now. He wasn't a bandit. He was a good chap. I know people who know him.'

'Grieco?'

'That's right.'

'I'm going to put a direct question to you. Would you like to see them all arrested?'

'No – no – no.'

'If one was on the run would you hide him in your house?'

'Well – I've got kids, you see.'

'I'll repeat my first question. What do the Tupamaros mean to you?'

'They're people with funny ideas.'

'Good or bad?'

'Good – but they'll never get them to work – not in this world. I think they're wasting their time.'

'Amongst the various things they've done, what impressed you most?'

'The exploit here at the Casino.'

'Why?'

'If I were to tell you it probably wouldn't be the truth.'

J A, 26 years old, small trader –
primary school to 4th year

'I'm apolitical. I've no idea about what you ask me. When I read about these things I think of it all as – well, fiction.'

'Have you never stopped to think what might be behind all these events reported in the newspapers?'

'No – why should I? I don't have any financial problems.'

'If you had financial problems do you think you'd be interested then in what's going on?'

'If I was hard up it's more likely that I might be – yes.'

'To summarise what you've said and what you haven't said it can be concluded that as far as you are concerned the Tupamaros are a political group whose aims are to change the conditions of life for people with economic or financial problems.'

'Now look here – I won't be involved. I'm apolitical, that's all.'

L S, 34 years old, housewife –
completed the full primary school course

'As far as I'm concerned I don't know. I don't know about them really. They do good and bad things. When they tried to give back the money they stole to the employees that was good. They're not bad for the poor because they don't take anything from them.'

'Would you like your son to be a Tupamaro?'
'No – it's too much of a sacrifice – too risky.'

DO, 30 years old, stonemason – full primary school course
'Do you work here in Maldonado?'
'I do now – but I work where there's work to be got. I've even been in Buenos Aires.'
'What do you think of the Tupamaros?'
'I think what they're doing is wonderful. They don't steal anything from me.'
'Do you think they're good just because they don't steal from you?'
'No – What I mean is that they don't steal from the poor. They rob banks and places where there's too much money.'
'And what do they do with the money?'
'They buy arms.'
'Why do they buy arms?'
'So as to be able to chuck the Government out.'
'Why should they want to overthrow the Government?'
'Because they don't go along with the Government's ideas. They have other ideas.'
'What sort of ideas?'
'I'm not sure – but at least they aren't Communist ideas.'
'What makes you think they aren't Communists?'
'Because the Communist Party has its own ways of doing things which are quite different. Besides the papers say – although I know the papers will say anything when it suits them – but they say that they had a photograph of Perón in the house where they were caught.'
'What does that mean?'
'A Communist isn't going to have a picture of Perón.'
'Would you say the Tupamaros are a right-inclined movement?'
'Lord no – I think they're more like Che and Fidel.'
'Do you think Che, Fidel and Perón go together?'
'People don't think so here, but in Argentina many people think they have similar aims.'
'Do you think the Tupamaros tend to lump them together too?'
'I don't know. I'm more inclined to think some escaped madman is behind them.'
'Do you think it's a widespread movement?'

'I can't say anything about that, but what I'm sure is that they only catch the little, unimportant chaps. The really big brains aren't found out.'

'Which of their activities has most impressed you?'

'The Monty affair. I did like it when they laid the account books of the place out on the Judge's doorstep. That was fabulous.'

'Which impressed you least?'

'What they said about kidnapping Batlle's kids. Though you never know if it was something made up by the police.'

Interviews taken in the town of Maldonado:

Z B, 19 years old, hairdresser – primary school

'What do the Tupamaros mean to you?'

'I don't like them.'

'Why don't you like them?'

'They're thieves.'

'Why do you think they want the money?'

'To have a good time.'

B Z, 43 years old, teacher

'What – in your opinion – are the Tupamaros?'

'At the moment they're the only hope for this country.'

'Just like that? Shall I write just what you say?'

'Just that.'

'Who did you vote for in the last elections?'

'The Nationalist ticket.'

'Don't you think that's a bit contradictory – after what you've been telling me?'

'No – because I don't think there is a real opposition. When the time comes they all – all the factions – act together.'

'You told me you're a primary school teacher. Which year do you teach?'

'Second year.'

'What do the children think of all this?'

'Well – anything which has the smell of adventure about it fascinates children of course. I set them to write out words beginning with the letter T. Nineteen children wrote down the word Tupamaro.'

A B, 25 years old, electrician –
primary school and technical school
'I think they're a bunch of delinquents.'
'Why?'
'All they've done so far is hold up places. They've done nothing effective. They say they want to start a revolution but they don't show much sign of doing it. There's something lacking. When the police flush them out they let themselves be picked up like little birds. Those aren't revolutionaries.'
'So you believe that to be a revolutionary one should resist the police violently?'
'Yes.'
'Don't you think that would just lead to a lot of useless deaths without forwarding the cause of revolution which you say they want?'
'When you want to force your ideas on people you can't afford to stop at small things.'
'So killing policemen you think is a small thing?'
'It's a small thing for a revolutionary movement.'
'You started off by telling me you thought them a bunch of delinquents and yet you criticise them as revolutionaries and object to their behaviour not being revolutionary enough.'
'That's right. What's the use of a revolutionary that doesn't act like one?'
'So you think then that in the case of a definite confrontation with the police the revolutionary should die, and kill somebody else.'
'Of course.'

The foregoing report was recorded outside a chemist's shop in the centre of Maldonado. A friend of the electrician's came up to see what was going on. He refused to give me any information about himself but was at some pains to explain why he didn't go along with the idea of killing policemen.

'The only proper attitude is to be passive. I believe that violence against the police is only justified if the police act to break up a definite – planned – political operation. But if all they happen to be doing is arresting a solitary member then violent resistance is not justified. If you died in those circumstances you don't do any good at all from the revolutionary point of view and, what's more, you create conditions where the police might abandon their present policy and begin to kill first and ask questions afterwards. Besides you can't discount the possibility of the police using the excuse of "resisting arrest" to inflict very heavy mortality on the revolutionary rank and file.'

'I can see you've thought the problem through very carefully.'

'Yes – I have.'

'Why won't you give me your name and so on?'

'You think you're talking to a member of the National Liberation Movement?'

'I'm sure if you were you wouldn't tell me.'

'Of course not.'

'What possibilities of success do you see for the movement?'

'Every possibility. History is on their side.'

'Despite the fact that they have recently suffered some serious setbacks?'

'For every man who falls five more join.'

C O, 22 years old, student at the School of Agriculture – reached 2nd year high school

'They are a revolutionary organisation.'

'What are their aims?'

'To impose a fairer régime on the country by force.'

'Which of the exploits they carried out seemed to you the most important?'

'The one at Financiera Monty.'

'Why?'

'Because they brought to light things which people ought to know about. It's very sad to see how the public is always deceived, led by the nose.'

'What criticism would you apply to them.'

'I don't know – none really.'

B Z, 19 years old, office worker – student at industrial school

'What do the Tupamaros mean to you?'

'I don't like politics. I don't understand what they want or don't want.'

'Fair enough. But do you think they are a political group?'

'Yes – but I'm not interested in the problem.'

T H, 20 years old, office employee –
  secondary education to 3rd year
'What do the Tupamaros mean to you?'
'What?'
'What do you think of them? Are they delinquents? Are they revolutionaries?'
'They're idealists.'
'Which of their exploits seemed to you the most important?'
'For them the one at the Casino.'
'I don't understand.'
'It's the one that was most fruitful from the point of view of what they're trying to do. The one at Financiera Monty was also important because it uncovered a lot that needed to be uncovered.'
'Which aspects of their activities would you criticise?'
'I don't know what the specific aim of each individual exploit is so I can't really give an opinion.'

At a café in the suburbs of Maldonado I questioned three old men who were standing in the doorway enjoying the sunshine. Two of them wouldn't give any information about themselves. They said they were against the Tupamaros' exploits and the intentions behind them. The third man, who said his name was B C, said he was retired and drew a pension from the Rural Pension Fund. He was 75 years old. His answer was: 'To me they seem just like the first Christians.'

April 1969

Go forth and set the world on fire

Ignatius Loyola

I believe in God
  Who created the Universe
  but not as a complete and finished thing
  as if it must thus remain for all time.
In God
  Who desires conflict between
  all living creatures,
  and change in all working conditions
  and political action.

85

I believe in Jesus Christ
  Who being 'a man alone – helpless',
  just as we all feel,
  still fought for change,
  changed everything,
  and was executed for it.

Dorothea Solle

Everything was just as it had always been – nothing had changed. The sad, cold, winter daylight filtered through the greeny-yellow glass of the windows in the dimly-lit chapel. Around me I could see the old familiar school-uniforms with their white collars. The same black stockings. The same slow, sleepy, fumbling gestures. In my day, I remembered, the cold faces were always heavy with tedium. So much used to be offered to us – in a dim, hazy future, in some other place and some other time. 'Life everlasting', 'Keep me from the temptations of the world – Oh Lord', 'Save me from its dangers and miseries', 'Keep me at all times from sin'. It seemed that in those days we were living in a world where we had little contact with anything. We were perpetually being 'kept from' things. It was always 'Save me from this' and 'Save me from that'.

Today the dim chapel looked just the same, so did the uniforms and white collars, but I listened in vain for the slow, monotonous voice of the priest to match the slow, monotonous tones in the depths of my memory, exhorting us, his daughters, to look to Saint Teresa for an example, to preserve our childlike spirit at all times and thus ensure total security and uninvolvement!

No such woolly, comforting words flowed over bored bent heads today. The priest spoke vigorously and his listeners in their blue uniforms and saintly collars were anything but bored.

'And I tell you that man can scarcely exert himself to search for God if his stomach is empty. Jesus took the earthly needs of man into account when he fed the multitude with the loaves and fishes – He knew that a hungry man is a blind, unaware creature, less than human and unable to seek communion with God.'

The sermon finished. The girls rushed helter-skelter into the yard. I approached the priest who, with bent head and a smile, was listening to the prattling chatter of a child of five or six.

I heard her say, 'I liked what you preached very much.' 'Did you? What did you like best?' asked the priest. 'The Communion Service – why is my friend Margarita allowed to take Communion and not me?'

As I watched the priest and the child I could hear a voice from the far distance of my childhood saying clearly, irrefutably: 'When you know the difference between the bread you eat and the Bread of Life. When you can distinguish between the two meanings – then . . .'

'When she can tell the difference between Bread and bread?' I asked the priest. He looked at me, smiled, stroked the child's head and said to her, 'All in good time – all in good time.' Then he turned to me saying, 'Do you really think it is enough to understand with the intellect that the Bread of the Eucharist is different from ordinary bread?'

'I don't know, I've never really thought about it.'

'What does the Eucharist mean to you?'

'I don't know that either. I've never thought about it seriously.'

'Nevertheless your reference to "Bread and bread" leads me to suppose that you were brought up a Catholic.'

'Indeed I was.'

'What did the Eucharist mean to you in those days then?'

'Are you asking what taking Communion meant to me?'

'Well – we could put it like that.'

'It meant having God on my side, for a few hours anyway. My conscience felt at peace. I was protected from temptation and sin.'

'Were there all that many temptations at that tender age?'

'We used to think there were. But nowadays? What's considered the proper age for a child to be confirmed, or to be given religious instruction?'

'Whenever he or she can understand fully the reality we are trying to convey through the Eucharist.'

'And what reality is that?'

'That there should be unity among men.'

'But isn't that just reiterating something that is already a fact? People are united nowadays.'

'The Eucharist doesn't just confirm something static and fairly acceptable, a sort of blessing on the *status quo*. It inspires to a unity which is quite different and by no means yet achieved.'

'And if the kind of unity the Eucharist proclaims can be attained through Communion, what should be the spiritual condition of a Christian who has just taken Communion?'

'When Communion achieves its essential significance the Christian should depart filled with renewed purpose to transform the conditions in which mankind exists.'

'Do you mean that true communion between men would lead to that?'

'Yes, people would be filled with a sense of commitment. They'd feel they must contribute to liberating – saving others.'

'Who said that?'

'Who said it? I don't know that you'd find a specific text about it.'

'All the same – I'd like to see it written down somewhere in a definite text, even if it was only a tiny bit in a long passage.'

'Well – there's the Gospel according to St Luke – the words "Unto you a saviour is born. I bring you tidings of great joy". A saviour – a liberator – it's all the same.'

'I don't know that it's all that clear, even now. What would "saving" or "liberating" have meant in the first century? Or for that matter what does it mean nowadays?'

'Exactly the same. You've got to start with the individual. Each and every one of us. To be liberated – or saved – simply means to slough off everything which prevents us being free – really free.'

'Prejudices, for instance?'

'Of course.'

'Economic differences? Insularity? Religious differences?'

'Yes exactly, you don't need to be careful about what you say. Christians will never find their true essence if they don't overcome the divisions within the Church.'

'If you can see that the Church is divided in itself how can this be overcome?'

'The Church needs to be reformed from the foundations up. Somebody said the old religious heaven is outdated, repressive. Mankind needs a new Heaven.'

'A new Heaven?'

'Don't sound so shocked. Does the word Heaven make you suspicious?'

'No – not really. I know we're not talking about a heaven somewhere outside the earth which takes no account of life here, nor of a substitute for the world. But tell me, what would a new, transmuted Church seek to bring about?'

'Communion with the Son of Man crucified.'

'But that's what it has always sought.'

'Not so – what was sought was communication with a god outside this world.'

'And now God is to be sought in this world?'

'Yes, and the Church now knows He is to be found in the hungry, the naked, the imprisoned – and on the lookout for the good deeds of good men.'

'What then would you say should be a Christian's mission?'

'To contribute to the liberation of others. That should be the first and essential commitment of the true Christian. You started this conversation by asking about when children should be taught the Catechism.'

'Yes – But I can imagine what your reply will be. You'll say that the age varies for each individual child and its ability to understand the deep significance of the commitment which the Christian must assume.'

'Would you accept that as a suitable criterion?'

'I think so.'

'Well then, let's take that as one criterion.'

'You mean there are others?'

'Yes – there are others. There are nine of us who live together and each one of us could have different ideas on the problem.'

'And do you all have a different view?'

'I didn't say that – I said we could have different ideas.'

'On such a concrete point?'

'Look – you must meet my friends. Come and lunch with us tomorrow.'

'Lunch?'

'Don't sound so surprised. Priests eat just like everybody else. When they can.'

The nine were sitting around a table on which was placed a large earthenware bowl full of steaming hot soup. The sun, shining through the grill over a high window cast a pattern on the worn, scrubbed wooden surface and made the jug of wine glow like a jewel. I guessed it would be rough, new wine, made from grapes.

I filled my plate with the aluminium soup ladle, broke the thick slice of bread and concentrated on my soup.

'You wanted to talk about the Catechism?' said one.

'If you really want to know, I want to hear what the opinions of the Third World Church are. I wanted to get them at source.'

'There's no specific Third World Church opinion.'

'Should I then have said Third World Jesuit opinion?'

'When you say "Jesuit"' – the young man who spoke had a strong Chilean accent – 'I . . .'

'Aren't you Jesuits?' I broke in.

'Yes – we're a section of the Jesuit Order.'

'A section which would rather be known for its future aims than for its past traditions,' said a voice on my right.

'And what are your aims?'

'To approach the socio-cultural problems of Latin America from a Christian conscience point of view.'

'When you say socio-cultural would you include the political aspects?'

'Of course.'

'A "Christian conscience approach" seems a pretty vague sort of concept – think of the disagreements within the Church itself.'

'You didn't let me finish. I was going to say a Christian conscience profoundly committed to change – or perhaps I should say willing to be committed to change.'

'And is this intention – or willingness – to be committed to change shared by all Jesuits?'

'The Company is profoundly divided.'

'Doesn't this weaken you as a group?'

'Yes, just as the Universal Church is affected on a different plane by the discrepant views of a Helder Camara and a Sigau,* or the position of Paul VI in the discourse of Medellin as compared with the Populorum Progressio.'

'We were talking of a Christian conscience committed to change. Was it you who said that?' I addressed a young man at the end of the table.

* Helder Camara, a bishop in the north of Brazil, an extremely poor part of the country. He maintained that the Church should sell off its vast wealth to give to the poor and return to a régime of poverty and austerity.

Sigau, a European Cardinal who advocates that the Church advance in the direction of extreme modernisation, not divesting itself of its wealth but allowing its priests more freedom, such as doing away with celibacy.

'No – I didn't say anything. I've just been listening.' He had a broad smile and an up-country accent.

'I thought it was you.'

'No matter – I listen and I agree entirely.'

'OK. I still think though that even if we add the words "committed to change" the idea of a Christian conscience still leaves one rather in the dark. How would this commitment show? What sort of action would be involved?'

'Are you asking how we would behave?'

'Yes.'

'That would depend on how each one feels the change should come about. What you're really asking is what means would be justified to bring about change. On that point I don't believe any two of us are in full agreement,' said one.

'You see – all of us here believe that one of the main aims of the Church should be to make man more conscious. There must be many ways of pursuing this aim, and all of them could be valid,' said another.

'Would you say then that one of the fundamental aims of the Church should be to make man more conscious?'

'I would prefer...' The priest on my right started to speak and then paused, lost in thought, his eyes gleaming behind the thick spectacles of the classic intellectual – he seemed the living embodiment of Ignatius Loyola's dictum 'Go forth and set the world on fire'. IT'S ASS

'I would prefer,' he repeated, 'that you say "One of the fundamental missions of the Church is to get the message of the New Testament across".'

'What is the message?'

'That man cannot seek to transcend – to realise himself – in a world where the Gospel is a thing apart, something outside daily life. Man will find God right here – God is working in history.'

'How?'

'Through Christ. The reality of Christ is transcendence made real – tangible.'

'I'm not with you.'

'Let's help you catch up. God, who transcends history, is nevertheless manifest therein through the humanity of Christ. God made flesh, made real.'

'How does that reality work in history?'

'By fermenting, questioning, drawing man towards full individu-alisation.'

'Let's revert to the duties of the Church. Would you say that one of its specific tasks is to make this Presence conscious?'

'Yes – the presence of what is transcendent, personal in history.'

'What was the Church's previous thinking on this point? Wasn't God always supposed to be among men?'

'If you could for a moment think of history as a kind of strip cartoon, you could say that the Church would generally place God right at the end of the story, outside history. Consequently man's journey through history could be brisk and uninvolved.'

'I don't understand.'

'What I mean is that man's attitude to the events of his time was considered unimportant. Of course this has to be smoothed down a little. The Christian has always had obligations towards the world.'

'"Love thy neighbour as thyself"?'

'Not exactly. "Love thy neighbour as thyself" is a basic precept, central to the New Testament. The obligations of the Christian a few decades ago were concerned with a more or less abstract morality – a code of things that could be done and things that should be avoided.'

'I'm not so interested in what ought to be avoided. Let's talk about the things to which the Christian was supposed to aspire.'

'Justice, charity, truth, love. All big, beautiful, abstract ideas, all airy-fairy – quite detached from the concrete realities of the moment. Christianity always did have strong leanings towards universality of ideas.'

'And that's all finished? Done with?'

He of the broad, up-country accent said, 'If you put it like that you're wrong. What you can say is that there are important groups within the Church seeking to put an end to that leaning towards the abstract.'

'You think the trend has been overcome.'

'Are you asking a question or making a statement?'

'I'm making a statement.'

'You're right,' he said, casting a swift glance round the other eight men whose ages ranged from 25 to 45. 'As far as we're concerned there's no longer anything abstract about love and justice.'

'How would love and justice be understood nowadays?'

'With reference to concrete facts and deeds. What matters is love here and now, and how to put it into practice. You've got to take real circumstances into account.'

'Could we say that without coming down to hard facts the word Love would have no meaning?'

'If you like.'

'And what would be the hard facts of helping a man here and now?'

'You'd have to start by specifying what sort of man you had in mind. A Bolivian tin miner is not the same as a German textile worker.'

'Let's talk about ourselves – us Latin Americans.'

'Love could be shown best by taking sides with those who are at present most oppressed, making common cause with them, by helping those who are in process of becoming conscious of this oppression.'

'Help them so that their consciousness may be clearer . . . so that they may become conscious more quickly . . .'

'Yes – thus the fight for liberation will gain in precision, determination, efficiency.'

'How would you reconcile "charity" with this new attitude?'

'There's nothing to reconcile. This *is* charity.'

'But we're talking about a socio-political task.'

'Yes – that socio-political task constitutes a more universal form of charity. What do you think charity is?'

'I'd better say what I think it used to be, according to the old saws I remember – it was bound up with philanthropy, compassion, giving alms.'

'Charity is to be a good neighbour to other men. To draw other men to you and get close to other people yourself; that's a really creative job. You don't find neighbours, you make them. To be a good neighbour is to work with that man and build a better world with him.'

'We've talked of making people conscious, of helping the oppressed, of liberating, of working for a better world. In fact there's just one question left to ask: how are we going to do all this?'

A great silence fell on the company – not, I feel, because my question had stumped them but because just then a large enamelled dish with a smoking hot, newly roasted lamb had been placed on the table. I reached out my plate and drew it back well filled with delicious-smelling meat and herbs. I forgot what I had asked. I confess I forgot everything except the food in front of me. A voice on my right startled me and made me drop my fork.

'You asked how we are going to do it? How a Christian should go about achieving these aims? You really want to know . . .?'

'I want to know, in fact, whether violence is permitted to him.'

'It would not be forbidden him.'

'On what basis would you say that violence is not forbidden to a Christian?'

'How would *you* contend that violence would be forbidden?'

'I could quote at great length but I'll choose what I think is the best-known saying, the one about turning the other cheek.'

'Christ's words should be understood within the context in which they were spoken. Moreover, though He may well have spoken once of offering the other cheek, He in fact never did offer it. With His hands tied behind him and surrounded by enemies He did not turn the other cheek, instead He said firmly to those who beat Him: "If I have done wrong tell me what I have done, and if I have done well, why do you beat me?" What do you think we were trying to say just now when we talked of concrete love, of love being shown by deeds? You agreed with that line of thought. I now wonder whether you really understood fully.'

'I'm not sure. I think so. You were trying to say that you can't love everybody equally; that you can't talk to humanity as a whole. That to love is to choose.'

'Yes, and what's more, to love one means that you have to discard another – loving one might even mean that you have to hate another. All love implies a choice.'

'I suppose Jesus throwing the Pharisees out of the Temple would be an example?'

'That's the episode that's always quoted when anybody wants to give an example of Jesus being violent, but there are nevertheless others less obvious but more illustrative of what I am saying. For instance the story of the Siro-Phoenician woman . . .'

'I'm quite prepared to talk about the Siro-Phoenician woman,' said the Chilean, standing up, 'but don't you think we can talk about her more comfortably over there by the coffee-pot? I'm afraid it's already getting cold.'

We all got up and went over to the table where the coffee was standing. The coffee was already tepid. 'Both the woman and us deserve hot coffee,' said the Chilean and departed kitchenwards bearing the coffee-pot.

'Tell me the story of the woman,' I asked the priest who had been sitting on my right and whose name I discovered was Mario.

'She asked Jesus to cure her daughter who was possessed of an unclean spirit. He replied "It is not right to take the bread from one's children and cast it to the dogs."'

'What did that mean?'

'That first He owed himself to His own people, the Hebrew people. And I tell you that when love is real it is also generally conflictive. You can't love everybody equally.'

'Nevertheless the most-quoted Bible texts are those in which Jesus appears as loving everybody indiscriminately.'

'Yes – because the Church wished to give Him that image, which served its purposes.'

'One of its aims was individual salvation – for this the Gospel was a panacea . . .'

'Exactly. There are ideas which, though extremely violent in context, become bland and innocuous out of context. Think of the words "I am the good shepherd". What sort of idea do they bring to mind?'

'I always think of a drawing of a good shepherd dressed in a blue smock with kind, translucent eyes and little lambs all around gazing up at him adoringly.'

'Nevertheless in the language of the day the words "I am a good shepherd" had a political significance. Although the expression was ambiguous – He was probably trying to avoid repercussions – what Jesus sought was to re-establish a leadership.'

'So you all find a political meaning to the "Good Shepherd"?'

'And how! Remember the way the prophets in Israel denounced those in public office. "Woe unto you, shepherds of Israel, leading the people to drink from contaminated water holes." But for centuries the Bible has been read in a neutral light, as an apolitical treatise. For centuries the Gospels were drained of concrete facts and filled with catechistic answers equally suitable for Africa, Asia and the Moon.'

'Conservatives, liberals, Mormons and witches.'

'Exactly.'

'Am I to understand that there is not necessarily any conflict between love and violence? And that, moreover, violence could be a manifestation of love?'

'You could understand it that way. I would prefer to say that Christian love is neither violent nor non-violent; each man, each generation has to create the deepest and most universal love he and they are capable of, with whatever means are at their disposal. This requires that every Christian should examine his love against the historical background of his time. So that the manner in which that love is exercised will depend on a judgement of reality which is bound to vary from individual to individual.'

'Who loves will be saved?'

'No – not if he doesn't use the means to convert that love into an effective love. Each man, each generation, must take stock of his or their resources and be responsible for choosing the most appropriate means of attaining the proposed ends. If the Christian comes to feel, after such due consideration, that the most suitable means for putting love into practice is by violence, he must not flinch.'

'But the concept of violence is so wide. To what extremes of violence may he go?'

'Shall we return to the Bible for a moment?'

'Please.'

'Let's turn to the Second Book of Moses – Exodus. Moses as a child was taken into Pharaoh's household and brought up to all the splendour appropriate to the high station of a pharaoh. One day when Moses had grown into a man, he witnessed an Egyptian beating a Jew, one of his brothers. Moses was overcome by rage, killed the Egyptian and hid the body in the sand. After a few days he realised that his crime had been discovered. To escape punishment he fled and hid.

'Jehovah appeared to him and told him to go back to Pharaoh and demand the liberation of the Jews. Moses did this but Pharaoh wouldn't listen to him. Moses united the slaves and tried to force the King to free them. He used various and violent means of bringing pressure to bear on Pharaoh but Pharaoh's heart was hardened and he would not free the slaves. Finally, and I'll read this to you straight out of the Bible' – the priest took the Bible up from the table and opening it, began to read from it –'"And it came to pass that at midnight the Lord smote all the first born in the land of Egypt, from the firstborn of Pharaoh that sat on his throne unto the firstborn of the captive that was in the dungeon, and all the firstborn of cattle. And Pharaoh rose up in the night, he, and all his servants and all the Egyptians; and there was a great cry in Egypt; for there was not a house where there was not one dead." And thus at last the Jews were liberated and able to leave the land of Egypt.' He closed the Bible, put it back on the table, and looking over his glasses said, 'The slaves recovered their freedom through a supreme act of violence on the part of God, who did not discriminate between the guilty and the innocent.'

'I'm surprised that episode hasn't been suppressed by the censor.'

'Wait until they find out about it.'

Part III

Enough! We Say

Operation Pando

Guns at the ready

At ten in the morning Antonio and I climbed on the bus. It was practically empty but we nevertheless chose the long seat at the back. Antonio had bought a morning paper but he didn't open it; he glanced at the headlines on the front page, folded it in four and put it in his pocket. We were both silent, applying ourselves to our self-imposed task of scrutinising every one of the passengers who boarded the bus. There was an old man dressed like a market gardener, two fat ladies loaded with parcels, a mother with three small children, several high-school children with their books under their arms, and some primary-school children. At Maronas, a young couple got on and sat in front of us. I looked them over as I'd looked over all those who had come aboard. She was wearing woollen slacks, dark glasses and a red silk scarf tied over her hair, and was carrying a tartan duffle bag from which protruded a Thermos. He was wearing grey trousers and a suede jacket. He put his right arm around the girl's shoulders and in his left hand he held some fishing-rods in a blue linen cover. I looked out of the window. It was a glorious day, the vivid green of the fields contrasting with the yellow of the flowering acacias. To sit under a willow tree waiting peacefully for a bite – how far away it all seemed, as if it belonged in another world. Alas for the sunshine – alas for the couple with their Thermos flask and fishing rods. I turned to Antonio to say something to him about the odd feeling of belonging to another planet, but Antonio was gazing fixedly at the blue cover of the fishing-rods which the boy had propped between his knees. I followed his glance – at the bottom of the cover the shape of a large gun butt was outlined against the tightly-stretched linen. We looked at each other and smiled. How many more of us were there? How many? That chap there in the checked shirt standing in the gangway. That thin, thoughtful boy sitting beside us. He was young, pale, well-dressed and looked at his watch from time to time. Those two girls chattering ceaselessly on the seat in front.

The bus slowed down and moved gently towards the right kerb. Antonio and I turned simultaneously to look out of the window.

The funeral cortège was already there and beginning to go by. At the head was the hearse smothered with wreaths, followed by six funeral cars with a few mourners. In the leading car a couple sat silent. He was dressed in dark blue and smoked, she held her head with her right hand and mopped her eyes with her left. I began to feel myself shaking with laughter and I pressed Antonio's arm. Nervously he gestured with his shoulder towards the other passengers in the bus. A respectful silence had descended on everyone. The men took their hats off, one of the women crossed herself. The young man beside us, oblivious to everything, continued looking into the distance, sunk in who knows what serious thoughts. For just a second, however, our glances crossed and I had the sudden and violent certainty that he was one of us. I turned away to look out of the window and did not look his way again.

Some days later I recognised his fine features, sad eyes, and lank dark hair in a photograph in the papers. He was Jorge Salerno. Within a few hours he was to be assassinated during the withdrawal from Pando.

Interview recorded later with the undertaker

'Well, I don't quite know how to say it. You couldn't really suspect anything. I mean, the person who came to make the arrangements was so . . .'

'So distinguished?'

'That's right, distinguished looking. He seemed a young man from a wealthy family.'

'Because of his clothes.'

'Oh everything, not just his clothes. His manners. He explained that it was a case of an uncle who had died in Buenos Aires, and it seemed to me the most natural thing in the world.'

'Quite. Why shouldn't he have an uncle who would die in Buenos Aires?'

'Exactly. Anybody could have, I mean to say. Well, I don't have uncles, but if I did . . .'

'How did he explain their wishing to bring him here?'

'He said that as he was the last of the direct line it was right to carry out the wishes of the dead man.'

'But why should the dead man wish to be brought here?'

'It seemed that he was from Soca and wanted to be laid to rest in the place where he had spent his childhood.'

'Was that what the young man said?'

'Yes. The old man had lived seventy years in Buenos Aires but he had always missed his own land. That's what he said. So they, his heirs, were going to fulfil his wishes.'

'Did they ask about the type of funeral they wanted, prices and so on?'

'Yes. The hearse was to be of a good type but not ostentatious. I immediately suggested they use the American hearse. I thought it ideal. It's classy without being luxurious, and completely closed in, as they wished.'

'Did he think it ideal?'

'Precisely.'

'Did he say so?'

'Yes, he said, "The very hearse Uncle would have chosen".'

'Then you discussed the funeral cars?'

'Yes. Six were required. Although there would only be twelve or fourteen people leaving from here, they needed six cars because they were going to pick up other relatives at Olmos Crossroads.'

'And, amongst all these arrangements, had they given you the name of the dead man?'

'Yes indeed. The name was the best part. Even if they had purposely chosen it?'

'Well, in fact they had.'

'Yes, yes, of course – what I mean is – it was well chosen.'

'What was it?'

'Antuñez Burgueno – don't you recognise it?'

'No.'

'The Antuñez own half of Pando and half of Soca.'

'Oh, I see, that was smart, wasn't it? It was a fitting name. And how much did the whole thing cost?'

'21,000 pesos, which they paid like gentlemen.'

'Like gentlemen.'

'Yes. Tell you the truth, I don't know what you'll think, but we have no complaints.'

'So you were at no time suspicious?'

'There was only one thing which seemed a bit – well, odd – that they brought back the coffin with the remains themselves. Usually it's the funeral company that arranges for the clearance through

Customs and so on. But in this case they brought the coffin right here to the undertaking parlour.'

'What was the coffin made of?'

'Lead.'

'And presumably they put a few bones in it.'

'Bones? Not likely. Arms, I'd say. But who would have thought it? They were so well-bred. You could see it a mile off. You should have seen how the niece cried as we started off. 8 October it was. She carried a bunch of flowers and she was crying like anything. The other one too – they both cried. Well – it's only natural – people always cry on these occasions.'

'Yes, of course.'

Presently I forgot about the young man next to us· I was deep in the subject which had been occupying my thoughts completely over the last few days. 'Penny for them?' said Antonio.

'I expect my thoughts are much the same as yours. How did you explain things to your wife – about going off like this today?'

'I told her I had to go to Aigua on an errand for the old man. And I told the old man to keep his trap shut because it was something to do with a bird.'

'And what did you tell your boss?'

'That I had a tooth giving me hell and I'd have to have it seen to in the morning so I'd be away until the afternoon.'

'D'you think you'll get back by three?'

'If it all goes according to plan, why not? I sometimes think the best thing would be to be on the run like you.'

'I haven't seen my wife for seven months. It's two years since I've played with my daughter. I often get news that "they" have been to the house and turned everything over and asked umpteen questions. I've imagined, at least a hundred times, how little Maria Elena would look with her large round black eyes and her stiff little plaits framing her face like parentheses. I can hear her saying in a firm voice, "No – he's not come home. I haven't seen him. I never see my daddy."'

I looked out of the bus window again. Incredibly the sun still shone. The couple in front were preparing to get off. Automatically I registered in my mind 'Kilometre 29 – they're going to enter Pando by an indirect route.' I fingered the gun I was carrying, tied a double knot in my shoelace and started to go over for the hundredth time all the details of the plan of what lay ahead.

Sitting under a tree at the side of the tributary road which meets Highway 8 at Kilometre 29, Diego, Gerardo and Ismael waited for their two companions who were due to meet them there at about midday.

As usual before an important exploit Diego hummed interminable, complicated tunes which none of us knew. 'Don't tell me none of you know any of Gardel's songs.' He smiled. 'I promise I'll learn "The Day You Love Me" for our next do.'

Gerardo checked his watch. Two minutes to twelve. 'What does your watch say?' asked Diego checking his own for the fourth time that morning. 'Time for Ana and Julio to arrive,' said Gerardo, zipping up his anorak. Ismael noted the movement and stood up, feeling the shape of his gun and two grenades through his coat. He took out and carefully put back the folded white handkerchief he would wear tied around his left arm during the operation, then raised both arms in salutation. Ana and Julio were coming slowly up the road, Ana carrying her tartan bag, Julio his fishing-rod. 'OK. Let's go,' said Gerardo, feeling a violent attack of butterflies in his stomach.

They didn't talk, they set off up the road. Diego and Gerardo went ahead, and about twenty yards behind came Ana and Julio; Ismael placed himself neatly half-way between, stopping now and again to imitate the song of some bird he could hear.

Ismael was the newcomer of the five. He had arrived at Cerro Largo some six months previously looking for work. At that time the sum total of his political education was a healthy mistrust of politics and politicians which he had had since childhood. It was a good start. Now, with four months' membership of the organisation under his belt he was a first lieutenant. A tireless worker, able to keep his cool at all times, he had a further attribute which, though not listed in the Good Guerrilla's Manual, was much appreciated by all his friends – he was cheerful and good-humoured.

It was 12.15 when they reached the outskirts of Pando. They had to mark time for half an hour or more. Without losing sight of each other they began to wander around. Gerardo was working out in his head – although he knew it was a silly pastime – the fact that of every ten people they passed, one was of their number. He mentioned it to Diego, who burst out laughing. 'D'you know what you've got?' he said. 'You've got delusions of grandeur. Pando has a population of 70,000. There'll be 50 of us all told when we take the place. 'Do your homework.' But Gerardo insisted; maybe he found the idea of 'one in every ten' reassuring. That's why, although he didn't really believe it, he went on: 'But I'm not talking about everybody. I'm talking about those in the street, at this moment.' 'Look,' said Diego, pointing out a plump little blonde with an attaché case in her hand who appeared to be gazing with rapt joy into the window of a shoeshop. 'Look, and cheer up; she could be one of your one in ten.' 'So she could,' thought Gerardo and looked at his watch again. Eight minutes to go. 'Come on,' he said, feeling the old, familiar butterflies in his stomach. 'Oh shit! I know if I could come into action with something in my belly I wouldn't get these pains inside every time I think about what I'm going to do.'

'Bullets don't go well with steak and chips,' said Diego. 'The well-trained, obedient guerrilla goes into action with his bowels evacuated, his stomach empty, and a card in his pocket showing clearly what his blood and Rh groups are, that's what. Stop grumbling. Come on.'

Before turning the corner Gerardo turned round. The blonde with the attaché case had left her window and was walking briskly towards the avenue.

Continuation of the interview recorded with the undertaker

'I went with the driver in the Catalina.'

'Wasn't it an American hearse?'

'No, at the last minute we sent a Catalina.'

'At the head of the cortège?'

'Of course – don't tell me you've never seen a funeral?'

'I've seen funerals – yes. Did you go along at a proper, funereal speed?'

'No – we kept up to the highway speed, about fifty.'

'And the mourners. Were they still very downcast?'

'Yes, the women were crying, the men were all very solemn and all properly dressed, in dark clothes.'

'The coffin with the remains was in the Catalina.'

'Yes, well, when you say remains . . . in a manner of speaking.'

'That's right, you said the coffin had arms in it.'

106

'That's right, although to be truthful I must say I didn't actually see them.'

'Of course, you had no occasion to see them.'

'No – none at all.'

'Did they put the coffin in the hearse themselves?'

'No, but they watched closely as the pallbearers put it in.'

'And you still didn't suspect anything?'

'On the contrary: I was very impressed. I thought of this man, the dead man, who must have been greatly respected, greatly loved. D'you get me? It was the attitude of the family. Later my impressions were confirmed.'

'Confirmed?'

'Yes, one of the nephews went with me and the driver in the hearse. He told us that the deceased had been a very extraordinary person. Greatly dedicated to charity and that sort of thing.'

'How long did it take you to reach the Olmos Crossroads?'

'An hour or so. When we arrived there were other relations waiting by the roadside. Six or seven of them.'

'Did they have flowers?'

'No, they didn't have any flowers, unless they had them in their bags. There wasn't one of them without a bag of some sort.'

'You're thinking that they had arms in the bags.'

'Of course, arms and whatever else they needed . . . leaflets.'

'Leaflets?'

'Yes, a lot of leaflets. At Pando we distributed leaflets like mad.'

'All of you? You too?'

'We were handcuffed to them – we had to go with them all over the place; well, I hardly know now what I'm saying.'

'It's natural, perfectly natural that you should be confused. You covered Pando with leaflets, is that so?'

'It looked like it to me.'

'What happened after Olmos Crossroads?'

'That's where the question of Uncle Pascual first came up. They began to say that Uncle Pascual was at Kilometre 40 and we'd have to go and pick him up.'

'And what did you do?'

'Us? We didn't do anything. We just went along.'

'And when you arrived at Kilometre 40?'

'There was a Volkswagen waiting. The chap got down and I

thought to myself, "That's no uncle." He looked too young to be an uncle, if you get me.'

'And he wasn't.'

'What do you think? They made us all get down.'

'At gunpoint?'

'No. They didn't have guns. They ran their hands over our clothes to feel for weapons, and then they put those special handcuffs they make on us. Have you seen them?'

'No, I've never seen any.'

'That's very odd. There's always photographs of them in the papers. They're home-made, out of wire. Well, at that stage they talked among themselves. They said they couldn't put us in the hearse because we wouldn't fit, or something like that. Anyway they finally put us in the Volkswagen van and once we were packed in we turned round towards Pando which was some ten kilometres back.'

'And what about the mourners' cars and so on?'

'Well, it seemed that they first took the hearse to the cemetery at Pando, where they left the flowers. That's what I heard. Meanwhile we in the Volkswagen van were going round here and there because it was early so we had to mark time.'

'Early for what?'

'For the assault.'

'How were you distributed in the van?'

'In front there was the driver and two others. In the back were our six drivers, me and three of them.'

'Did you talk?'

'Of course.'

'What did you talk about?'

'All sorts of things.'

'About what they were going to do in Pando?'

'No.'

'Politics?'

'A bit. You know . . . they always explain things, it's their way.'

'What do they explain?'

'You're a journalist and you don't read the newspapers? They explain why they do this or that and how they plan to stop injustice, set the world to rights, all that. They always explain everything.'

'That means they weren't nervous . . . if they could bother to go in for long explanations.'

'No – I don't think they were nervous.'

'What about you? All of you?'

'Were we scared?'

'Yes, were you nervous?'

'Would you be nervous talking to three lads who could have been your sons? We weren't bothered.'

Fifteen minutes to go. Antonio, me and the other two making up the commando, we'd taken up our positions around the bus station, 80 metres from our objective, waiting for zero hour. I looked at my watch. Ten minutes to one. Half of Pando would be eating its midday meal at that time. I ran a rapid eye over our party. Propped against a pillar Antonio had the newspaper he'd bought earlier opened out and was pretending to read. A few metres away from him, practically on the edge of the kerb, Guillermo was telling Snub-nose, in enthusiastic tones which would have stirred the very stones in the road, all about that goal that Spencer had muffed during the last game. I smiled inwardly. To any unsuspecting bystander who might have noticed the pair, Snub-nose appeared to be enthralled by Guillermo's vivid description. I knew that in fact he could have absolutely no idea of what Guillermo was saying to him, that his eyes and his whole attention were concentrated on a point some 80 metres behind Guillermo!

I took out some tobacco, rolled a cigarette and started to smoke, slowly. I felt calm. For three days we had kept watch on the fire station which was our objective, and the four of us were agreed that if the taking of the police station – which was to precede the fire station action by a couple of minutes – went smoothly, the job with the firemen would be easy. I looked at my watch. Six minutes to go. Two impressive funeral cars with their half-drawn velvet curtains turned the corner and drove slowly towards the banking area of the town. Seconds later a third went by, then a fourth drove sharply around the plaza. On the corner by the police station Weepy was already at his post. Thin, tall, grave, engulfed in his funeral attire, he was an exemplary mourner. Nobody could possibly imagine that he had done anything in his life except attend wakes. I could see in my mind's eye the pistol on his right hip, and then, just as I used to think up thrilling stories for myself when I was a child, I imagined him putting up both arms and crying out 'Pando is ours'.

A fifth mourners' car approached and carried straight on. I recognised the man at the wheel. I lowered my head, inhaled a great mouthful of smoke and looked at my watch again. In thirty seconds the commandos in charge of attacking the police station would go into action.

One o'clock sharp. We saw our friends walk through the door of the police station and we started slowly to cross the road.

Evidence of a police officer

It was about one o'clock when a man and a woman came into the station and asked for the Police Chief. I said he wasn't in and went to the back to inquire. When I came back I found myself looking into their guns. They were telling me to put my hands up. I laughed because I thought it must be a joke, but I saw several chaps in Air Force uniforms, one with a sub-machine-gun, and heard one of them say 'Hands up! You're all covered.' They made me go through to the yard where I found other officers in the same position. One of the sergeants had had his glasses taken from him and when he said he couldn't see anything, they replied that he wasn't there to see anything, and that the less he saw the better, but they gave him back his glasses, tucking them into his pocket.

From where I stood in the yard I saw Sergeant Olivera coming out with his revolver all set to do battle with them. Three people fired at him. They put him in a room. He tried to resist but they threatened to blow him up with the grenades. Olivera surrendered. He was wounded in the arm. They tied our hands with copper wire and all of us, about ten, were put into the cells and made to face the wall. The man in charge said, 'Bring the parcel in carefully', as if it were a bomb or something that they put in the middle of the cell. But they took it away immediately and set a woman to keep watch over us, telling her that at the slightest move on our part she should shoot. She said there'd be no problem.

At that moment they brought Chief of Police Cabrera to the cells with the Deputy-Chief Floro Caraballo. They tied their hands behind them and made them face the wall along with the rest of us. The man who brought the Chief in shoved a gun in his neck and said, 'Do you remember when you searched my house?' Somebody explained to him that it hadn't been Cabrera but the previous chief, so the man took his gun away and said, 'Keep quiet, Fatso, don't go doing anything silly because nothing is going to happen to you.' The girl stayed for a while guarding us and then locked the door on us from outside, but she didn't put the padlock on; then she left, saying we were to stay where we were without moving for ten minutes as there'd be a guard upstairs. There wasn't a sound. When we finally got out with the help of some neighbours, we wanted to go after the miscreants but realised we had no arms and we had to start by asking for arms around the neighbourhood.

We ran to the Banco Republica but they had already withdrawn. We could hear the sound of gunfire coming from different quarters. We drew up an inventory of what had been taken and found we were short of a dozen guns, four sabres, two truncheons, five police caps, three police jackets, three police coats and four pistols.

We saw our friends go into the police station and very slowly we began to cross the road. Eighty metres separated us from our objective. It would take us one minute to cover them. If everything went well that one minute would be sufficient for the police station to be occupied.

The bus-stop teemed with people. We advanced more or less together. We had covered some 30 metres when we heard the sound of shots. For a fraction of a second we stopped and looked at each other. Something had gone wrong at the police station. The glass from a window splintered on the pavement. The fireman on watch at the entrance to the fire station looked up, surprised and made as if to go in and investigate, but he held back. He glanced again at the window and, obviously deciding it couldn't be anything of importance, he returned to his post. Without stopping I looked towards the bus station but couldn't tell whether the people there had heard the gunfire or not. We reached the door of the fire station swiftly overcame the guard and pushed inside. By this time we all had our guns in our hands and the white handkerchiefs round our arms to avoid confusion. Antonio kept watch by the door and the rest of us ran to the back of the building. We crossed a deserted yard and went into the sleeping quarters. Five or six men were having a siesta. When they saw us come in armed they remained paralysed on their beds, more, I think from sheer surprise

from fear. We didn't waste a moment, we ran our hands over
looking for arms and then pushed them out into the yard,
ng them turn to face the wall. I heard Guillermo saying,
we're Tupamaros and we're taking Pando, nothing'll happen to
you, we'll just hold you for a while.' Meanwhile I'd run to the
lavatories. A giant of man was urinating, his back turned to the
door. 'Hands up!' I shouted. He laughed and went on peeing. I
repeated the order, poking the gun into his ribs. The penny
dropped and without turning he lifted his arms above his head. I
made him go into the yard and stand like the rest, facing the wall.
The situation was under control. But there seemed to be a problem
at the police station where we could hear more gunfire. Something
was wrong. We quickly agreed between ourselves that we ought to
go and help, but just then one of our chaps put his head over the
wall at the bottom of the yard separating the fire station from the
police station and called out: 'Don't worry, everything's fixed.'

At the two stations everything was quiet and under control. The
problem was now out in the street where people, alerted by the
sound of bullets, had gathered in alarm and were looking around
for any policemen who might be near.

Guillermo and I, who just a couple of minutes before had been
preparing to go over to the police station, now ran instead to the
door. Two policemen with their guns in their hands were running
up the middle of the road. We went towards the kerb, shielding
ourselves behind a column. The policemen stopped and made signs
to us to approach. We in turn invited them to approach. If we
hadn't had guns in our hands, it might all have seemed some sort of
game. But they and we knew that it was no game. The people in
the street, however, didn't seem to realise this. They milled
around – beside us, in front of us, behind us, everywhere; people
everywhere, curious, unafraid, unaware that death might be un-
leashed amongst them at any moment.

A shrill voice cut through the heavy silence which had fallen on
the scene. 'It's the Tupamaros, it's the Tupamaros! They're
taking Pando.'

I saw astonishment on the faces of the two policemen, saw them
back away slowly and disappear behind the doors of a shop. This
wasn't, however, the end of the problem. More and more people,
anxious not to miss anything, crowded the pavements, stood on
doorsteps, hung over balconies. In the distance shots could be

heard. In a few short minutes the various actions would have been completed and the most difficult of all operations would begin – the ordered withdrawal. We needed the streets to be clear, not packed with inquisitive spectators who would get in the way of our retreat. We yelled at them to go away but they backed away a couple of paces and there they stuck. We threatened them with violence, waving our guns at them, our faces grim, but all they did was to run around in small circles and then they'd start coming up close again. We later discovered that it had been like that all over Pando. The people, friendly or annoyed, impatient or sympathetic, careless of the guns we carried, kept getting under everybody's feet, wanting to see, protesting, approving, asking questions, sometimes even helping. They were a damned nuisance.

Evidence of a member of the fire brigade

It must have been five past one when a couple came in and said they wanted to make a call. I showed them the phone booth. Right after them several men came in who said they were from Intelligence and Coordination and showed me a card which I didn't look at as I didn't have my glasses – I can't see without my glasses. The one who seemed to be in charge ordered all the employees to go to a room at the back whilst they searched the premises for a bomb which had been reported and which was said to be in the engine bay. I was the last one left when a policeman came running in asking to use the phone because he said the police station had been attacked by the Tupamaros. The man in charge of the group who were escorting us out to the back room told the policeman that they were Tupamaros too, and made him hand over his gun, which he did. We all went to the room at the back and were made to stand with our faces to the wall except for a female worker who was pregnant and was allowed to sit down. Once we were all shut in, one of them told us they belonged to the National Liberation Movement and that we should keep calm and nothing would happen to us.

Several of the female employees got nervous and started to scream. The woman with the white fur jacket, who had come in first and asked to use the phone, opened a bag and drew out a submachine-gun and told us that if we did not shut up they'd have to use different tactics.

After about five minutes they said they were withdrawing but we were forbidden to leave for another ten minutes. Our door had not been bolted, only the doors to the engine room and the operations room. When the ten minutes were up we went out to tell the police, and then we found that the whole of Pando had been taken.

At ten minutes to one we were all in the Plaza at Pando, ready for the assault. Ana and Julio were sitting on a bench; to all appearances they were a carefree, happy couple on holiday. Ismael and Diego were walking up and down deep in conversation. Gerardo, with a deceptively absent-minded air, gazed at the trees and for the tenth time that morning felt his pistol. The safety catch was already off and a bullet was in the breech.

As was usual with him he could now think of the impending action without a tremor from his stomach. As usual during the last few minutes he was assailed by a feeling of hunger and the complete and absolute certainty that everything would go well. He took a mint out of his pocket and began to suck it. Eating a mint before going into action didn't rate as a violation of the regulations, he thought, and smiled at his stupid idea. He never knew why at such times he always had stupid ideas. He glanced quickly over to the left of the Plaza and saw that the black funeral car was still there. Inside the four chaps who made up the commando sat wearing the grave faces suitable to a funeral cortège. At a few seconds past one o'clock a man waving a white handkerchief indicating the start of the action would cross the avenue on a roaring motor-cycle.

It was just one o'clock when, over to the left, the violent roar of a motor-cycle engine burst into life and the waving handkerchief they were waiting for flashed by.

Those in the plaza stood up and began to walk towards the Bank of Pando. The black funeral car started up its engine and waited for a few minutes. Everybody had to go into the bank at the same time. Whilst Ana, Julio and the others walked along the pavement, the funeral car slowly passed them. The members from the funeral car would enter the bank through the door on Street 'A'. Those on foot would go in through the door on Street 'B' just round the corner. The car stopped in front of the bank. Four men got down and started to cross the road. A passer-by saw them and seemed to realise intuitively that something odd was going on. It could have been that he noticed the shape of the sub-machine-gun concealed under Gabriel's coat, or it could have been just the expressions on the men's faces. The man who was passing knew that these couldn't be ordinary customers and tried to go back, cross over – and most likely give the alarm. He was quickly surrounded and made to go into the bank. A pistol which nobody could see but which he could feel rammed against his ribs immobilised him for a few seconds.

Meanwhile Gabriel went ahead, he vaulted over the counter with his sub-machine-gun in his hand and announced that they were members of the National Liberation Movement and were taking over the bank. 'Keep quiet and face the wall,' he commanded. Everybody then set to their appointed task.

Diego and Ismael went to the strongroom, preceded by the manager. The doors were open. They didn't even have to say 'Open Sesame'; the strong room gave up its 8 million pesos without a murmur, it was just a case of putting it all into bags. In a minute and a half they'd finished.

Meanwhile clients were coming into the bank and these, prompted by Gerardo, raised their arms and faced the wall. One woman came running to the bank stopped in the door and screamed, 'They're holding up the Banco Republica.' Then she saw Julio standing a couple of feet away pointing a gun at her. 'What, here as well?' She laughed. Julio nodded and laughed too.

Ana started to distribute leaflets. Some people, although holding their hands above their heads, still somehow managed to read what was on them. Ana, encouraged by their interest, started to explain the aims of the Tupamaros.

The absurdly normal air of calm which prevailed despite guns, leaflets and the bags containing millions of pesos, was abruptly shattered by the wail of a siren. For a few seconds everything and everybody froze into immobility. Ana stopped talking; Ismael lifted his bag which he clasped to himself like a baby; Diego stood rigid, his bag hanging, a look of annoyance on his face; Gerardo and Julio had raised their guns very slightly whilst they looked around with grim faces. 'Keep cool,' said Gabriel as he lowered the counter-flap. 'Nothing's happening – it's just the Banco Republica's alarm signal.'

The moment of suspended animation passed. Everything got into gear again and started to move. Ana went on talking as she backed towards the door, scattering the last of the leaflets. Diego continued on his way. Later he was to explain to Ismael that the siren had not frightened him at all but that he had an irrational hatred of strident noises which stunned him like running head-on into a brick wall. Everybody was ready to leave. Outside the door Jorge was talking to an old lady in a large hat and big grey muffler. She waved a paper under Jorge's nose, Jorge in turn was waving a Colt revolver which he did not bother to hide. 'But I've got to collect my pension – it said in the newspaper that today was the day for my group.' 'Yes, ma'am,' screamed Jorge into her deaf ears, 'but you can't collect today. The bank has been taken over by the Tupamaros. Go inside – it's dangerous out here.' He repeated the words, talking as loudly as he could in her ear, but she didn't move. 'Will they pay me tomorrow, do you think?' she asked. 'I'm sure they will but do go inside now,' he said. As she still didn't move Jorge grasped her by both shoulders and pushed her into the bank, and all the time she kept on muttering, 'I don't know why you make me come in here if they aren't going to pay me today.'

Ismael, doubled up with laughter, had rested the bag on the floor. 'OK, let's go!' said Gerardo, waving his pistol. Jorge pushed him back. Behind the funeral car a policeman was crouching; he had his gun trained on the door of the bank, covering the escape. Julio, who was the best placed to do so, opened fire. The shots hit the car but did not touch the policeman who continued firmly at his post. 'Shit,' said Gerardo. 'It's ten past one and they're all waiting for us.' Diego, his face all crinkled up and his eyes narrowed, snatched the sub-machine-gun from Gabriel and aimed. Ismael and Ana leapt on him. 'Calm down,' said Ana. 'Don't forget that we brought the guns to inspire a healthy respect, not to use them.' 'In an extreme situation we have to use them,' said Gabriel, flattening himself against the wall as a bullet scraped his overcoat. He took his pistol out of his pocket and began to fire as well.

The exchange of shots lasted for four minutes at the end of which time the policeman lay wounded on the ground. They all made a dash for the car which was riddled with bulletholes like a sieve. The policeman seeing them running towards him cried, 'Don't kill me. Please don't kill me.' 'And why should we kill you, imbecile that you are, son of a thousand whores?' snapped Gerardo, pushing him roughly aside.

Julio took the wheel. Eight anxious faces watched his hand as he turned the starter. A tremor shook the old funeral car, then the hoarse, welcome sound of the engine burst forth greeted by a heartfelt cheer. Ana threw the very last leaflets out of the window. They floated slowly around the car. They were off.

The policeman, painfully dragging one leg, crossed the road, reloaded and fired. He fired several times until he hit one of the wheels of the fleeing car.

With their tyres flat, zig-zagging along the road, they reached the road to the cemetery. When the others saw them coming they started up their cars. Those arriving had to fire in the air to signal to the others to wait for them. They abandoned the now useless car and distributed themselves as best they could in the other cars.

Gerardo, one of the few of this particular commando unit who was to escape imprisonment or death within the next few hours, explained to one of his friends later: 'That was when we lost our identity as a group. We got into several different cars. We didn't know anybody. We didn't know who were officers and who were other ranks. Nobody knew whom to obey. This was our undoing when presently we were caught in the police net at Toledo Chico.'

Evidence given by an eyewitness at the Bank of Pando

It was one o'clock. Six or seven armed people came into the bank. One of them jumped over the counter. They said they were Tupamaros and that we should keep calm because they were workers just like us. In a few minutes they took all the money out of the strongroom. They called the manager and chief cashier by their names. They asked the manager to hand over his car keys and the gun he carried. Then they sent us, with our hands up over our heads, to a back room where there's a kind of store with a door to the outside which is unlocked. When they were leaving they told us they had taken the police station and the Banco Republica. The whole thing was over in three minutes.

Continuation of interview with the undertaker

'So you and the six drivers . . . what was your position?'

'I was in charge of the funeral cortège. I don't know whether you know it, but our company always sends a senior undertaker to be in charge of the proceedings.'

'I didn't know. So the six were put into the van.'

'Yes, we began to go round and round because it was too early for the assault.'

'Which of the assaults?'

'Our lot was the Banco Republica.'

'But you didn't see anything of the action ...'

'How could we? They didn't let us. Before getting down they told us to keep quiet.'

'Who told you to keep quiet?'

'One of them, the one they called Pedro. From the sound of his voice he'd be very young.'

'Why from the sound of his voice? Couldn't you see them?'

'We were made to look down all the time so that we wouldn't see their faces.'

'And how did the assault go?'

'Fantastic. In a few minutes they got 40 million. They only had one bit of bad luck. One of the girls, she fired by mistake and hurt one of her friends in the stomach. They had to take him to hospital in a hurry so that he could be operated on.'

'A hospital in Pando?'

'What do you mean, a hospital in Pando? No, one of their own hospitals that they have hidden away – God knows where.'

'But except for that everything went well?'

'Yes, very well indeed. It seems that inside one of the banks one of them stood on the counter and gave a speech.'

'You read about that afterwards in the papers?'

'No, we heard when the boys who were with us got back in the car because they were teasing the one who'd made the speech. They were telling him he should go into politics and if the people in the bank hadn't had their hands up they would certainly have applauded.'

'What did he say?'

'He laughed.'

'They were all quite cool then?'

'Just like you and me.'

'Who took the wounded man – did you?'

'No – we took the millions! They threw the bags in on top of us; just think, to have 40 million thrown at you – just like that! No, the wounded man was taken in another car.'

'Which other car?'

'There were two cars involved in this particular assault: the van with us in it and some of them, and a funeral car. I don't know how many there would have been in that.'

'Where were you all when the Republica alarm went off?'

'Practically at the door of the bank. We were just moving off.'

'And what happened?'

'All hell broke loose – you could hear horns blowing, shots being fired, and the siren.'

'And what about them?'

'They were as cool as if nothing at all was happening. Us – we from the funeral company – we were a bit nervous I can tell you, but not them. They were throwing leaflets about and blowing the horn like mad because people were swarming around in the middle of the road and we couldn't get through. It was like some sort of a show. They kept yelling "Long live the revolution!" One of us who managed to get a look out said there were lads wearing white armbands directing the traffic.'

'Tupamaros?'

'What do you think they'd be – boy scouts? All those wearing a white armband that day in Pando were Tupamaros.'

'Did you go back to Montevideo with them?'

'No – soon after we left the cemetery they made us get out as the cars were too heavily laden.'

'Were you still wearing handcuffs?'

'No, they took them off, then they thanked us.'

'Thanked you? What for?'

'I don't know. They just said "Thanks for everything."'

The convoy set off. There was a festive air about the whole exploit now. They were all exuberant, indomitable.

Dishevelled, their faces red and shining as if they had just been taking part in some exciting, competitive sport, laughing and talking all at once, piled higgledy-piggledy in the funeral cars, they presented an unusual picture, impossible to fit into any known setting.

They travelled the first few kilometres in this buoyant mood, telling each other absurd or funny stories, behaving as if drunk.

Only the leaders of each group seemed to escape the general lunacy. They were easy to place. All eight of them were silent, concentrating, alert, divorced from the prevailing boisterousness and euphoria of victory which enveloped all the others.

Gerardo, silent, sitting next to the driver of one of the funeral cars, tried to control the pains in his stomach which now gripped him continuously. He dug his nails into his palms and kept ramming his right foot down on a non-existent accelerator. His whole attention was painfully concentrated on the speedometer which didn't go beyond seventy, couldn't in fact, with any degree of safety, exceed that speed. He had a presentiment that something would go wrong. He turned to his companion on the right, a very fair young man with a smooth, practically beardless face, who had been chatting, singing and laughing ever since they'd left Pando. 'Do you know, I have a feeling that the police are surrounding us.' The youngster stopped talking and laughing as if he were mad. Then, frowning, he looked out anxiously. A patrol was coming along the road marching slowly. The policemen touched their caps with one finger as a signal of respect. Gerardo relaxed. He was an idiot to talk about his intuitive momentary fear, spoiling the fun of somebody who had until then been in the heights of euphoria. 'I'm sure I'm wrong,' he added smiling, with the intention of comforting the boy. He's very young, he thought to himself. He can't have done his military service yet. The boy didn't smile. He took the handkerchief off his arm, folded it carefully and with a serious expression, looked at Gerardo again. Gerardo knew what the look meant and hastened to apologise. 'I've been a member of the organisation for four years,' said the boy. 'I'm terribly sorry,' said Gerardo, 'I thought you couldn't be older than twenty.' 'I'm twenty-four,' said the boy with a hard look.

Eusebio, in the Volkswagen, was also silent and thoughtful. A patrol, the third within two kilometres, had just gone by. The last two had been travelling at speed and in the opposite direction to theirs. They've known for some time but they must think we are still on the outskirts of Pando, he thought. At that very moment Antonio turned and pointed to the patrol car which had just passed. 'What do you think?' Eusebio asked. 'I think they know but are confused – they must believe we're still hanging around Pando,' said Antonio. 'I think so too,' replied Eusebio.

'We need six minutes,' Diego was saying in another of the funeral cars. 'Just six – let's take it that the Montevideo police found out twenty minutes ago. They must still be giving orders and planning action. When everything is ready to go, we shan't be anywhere around.'

He was wrong. Two minutes later, a little short of Cassarino, near the city boundary of Montevideo, the members of a police patrol saw them coming and crouched behind their car as if to shoot. But they didn't dare fire. The funeral cortège, driven – apparently – by uniformed chauffeurs and with policemen sitting in some of the funeral cars, nonplussed them.

From then on everybody in the convoy was plunged into gloomy silence. They were sure now that the police were on to them, and moving. To avoid a confrontation might be just a matter of minutes.

They drove quickly into Montevideo. On the corner of Andaluz and Castanas Streets, in a quiet suburban area, the convoy divided into three groups taking different directions. Nearby at different places, two of the groups transferred their arms and the men wanted by the police into ordinary private cars. Those not on the run started to walk along, separately, looking for a bus or taxi.

Antonio walked some 500 metres to the avenue where he caught a bus, sat down and opened the paper he had bought that morning and which this time he really began to read. At twenty to three the bus deposited him opposite his office. He bought a sandwich at the corner shop, ate it hurriedly before going in to work. His boss greeted him as he went in. 'How's the tooth?' 'Better, thanks,' said Antonio making a show of rubbing his face with his left hand while he signed on with his right. He expected a phone call from Pedro before three to confirm that everything was in order. At ten minutes to three the phone rang. 'Antonio?' 'Yes.' 'All OK. We're still short of three boxes of books which must be about to arrive any time now. As soon as they get here I'll let you know.' 'OK. Thanks.' He sat down, opened his calculating machine and settled down to work. Half an hour later a colleague rushed in from the street. 'Have you heard there's been a frightful shindy with the Tupamaros?' 'No,' said Antonio innocently. He waited cheerfully for the other man to tell him something about the Pando exploit, but what he heard was: 'They're shooting it out with the police at Toledo Chico.'

A few days later, Gerardo, one of the few who escaped the trap at Toledo, told a group of his friends: 'We were proceeding along the road as planned – the two funeral cars and the Volkswagen van. We didn't by then have either arms or any of the wanted people with us as we'd already transferred those to the private cars as arranged. We were very near to where we would abandon our vehicles and would carry on, on foot, individually, unarmed, looking for some form of public transport.

'In front of us was the other funeral car driven by Roberto. It was still loaded and due to meet its contact – a private car – less than a kilometre farther on. The van was immediately behind us, it had already transferred its load, the money and arms, to Tito's little lorry which was following farther behind along the same road until it got to the crossroads where it would turn off and go into the city through a maze of suburban roads.

'We were two kilometres and two minutes short of the outlying suburbs of the city, around us were fields and smallholdings and patches of common land. Just another two minutes and we could have slipped away and disappeared. And then, turning a sharp bend which completely obstructed our view of the road ahead, we ran slap bang into them. First one patrol car and then a second slewed across the road blocking it. We realised it was hopeless to try to put up a fight. Only six of us were armed and we were facing desperate odds. We tried to turn the cars so as to shoot out of the back while trying to escape the way we had come, but the road was too narrow, with high banks on either side. The only one to get away was the little lorry coming along at the tail of the convoy, which managed to turn and flee into country lanes where the police had not yet set up roadblocks.

'The rest of us decided to abandon the vehicles and scatter. Try to lose ourselves in the surrounding fields. Few of us knew each other. Disorder reigned. The commandos had dispersed as a result of the breaking down of the cars at Pando, and this weakened us as a group. We didn't know what to expect from anybody. We didn't know who were officers and who were other ranks. We didn't know whom to obey. We made a dash for it in twos and threes into the flat countryside which offered very little cover.

'Armoured cars, army lorries, patrol cars, and two helicopters flying so low they nearly scalped us, rounded us up relentlessly. Hooting, shots, orders shouted through loudspeakers filled the air with hideous din. Pandemonium reigned.

'Although each one of us individually was convinced we were all going to be massacred nobody said anything about it. I began to hate the sun which spotlighted with dazzling brilliance every inch of the terrain where we were playing out our desperate parts. Nothing could move, not a leaf could stir, without being instantly detected.

'Screaming voices emanated from the air, pinpointing movements and directing manoeuvres. Through the windows of the few houses inside the police cordon shadowy faces could be seen, eyes gaping wide with fear and astonishment. The police became a single, blind, bloodthirsty beast. Anything human which happened to move within the net was kicked, beaten and driven with blows from rifle butts into the prison vans. The persecution could only be classified by one word – hysteria.

'Though there may have been few outside witnesses, the bodies of the three Tupamaros* were a mute and devastating indictment. Caught unarmed, they were killed as they surrendered. Bullets were poured into their bodies long after they were already dead. One of them had 30 bullets in his body and after that they had bashed his skull in with their rifle butts.

'Rumour had it that Sendic, dressed as a farm worker, had been concealed by a family in the area. In fact Sendic, dressed quite as usual, had been driving the little lorry which had turned tail swiftly and escaped like an eel through the gaps in the police cordon.'

Text of one of the leaflets distributed in Pando

FACTS THE PUBLIC SHOULD KNOW

A few months ago three students and a worker were assassinated at Manslava. Now a bank worker has died, victim of the sick fury turned on the Union (after the end of the strike) by reactionary diehards like Francese, encouraged by the Régime, whose sole aim is to humiliate the workers.

There is no freedom of opinion. Newspapers, radio

* Jorge Salerno, Alfredo Cultelli and Ricardo Zabalza.

programmes and political parties are suppressed, Parliament is helpless.

Hundreds of detainees fill the prisons and the military barracks.

Men are dismissed in great numbers from their jobs by government decree, causing hundreds of families to be thrown on the bread line.

The unions and the right to strike have been trampled underfoot.

Torture and beatings are inflicted with complicity of the Judiciary.

People are tried and imprisoned without proof of guilt.

The incomes of the great majority are frozen whilst an increase in affluence of a small minority is encouraged.

The country is being sold out to foreigners.

Corruption is rampant in the Government.

Montaner was appointed a minister despite being involved in the illegal sale of truckloads of cattle.

Charlone and Sanguinetti continue as ministers although implicated in the EFCSA frauds.

Peirano Facio, whose name was linked with the manipulation of Banking and the Meat Industry, continues to enjoy the confidence of the murderer Pacheco [the then President of Uruguay].

The names of Frick Davies, Pereyra Reverbel and others were listed in the books of Financiera Monty.

Bartolome Herrera continues as Treasurer although involved in the graft scandals.

Jorge Batlle and several others continue free although their part in the malpractices last year was fully proven.

Faced with all this there are only two lines open to us. We knuckle down and put up with things as they are, or we revolt and resist.

We preach and follow the second line, true to Artigas and those Tupamaros who in the past have fought to the death.

We too can imprison those responsible for this situation such as Gaetano Pellegrini.

We raid the homes of compliant politicians just as they raid the workers' homes.

We snatch the arms we need from the enemy.

We do not turn to foreigners to ask them to finance the revolution.

We take the funds we need to mount the revolutionary apparatus from the enemy.

Although they try to muzzle us our voice will continue to be heard, by means of leaflets such as this one, by radio announcements, by seizing a town if necessary, as we have done today.

The fight is only just beginning. It will be long and tough. We offer this way to those who consider themselves true Uruguayans.

Our exploit today is offered as a homage to that great American, Che Guevara, assassinated two years ago today in Bolivia – as a tangible proof that his fight was not in vain.

BY THE C.I.A.

Pando

8 October 1969
National Liberation Movement
Che Guevara Commando

A few days after Operation Pando the Minister of the Interior issued the following communiqué:

As from today none of the communications media in the country may use any of the following terms: cell, commandos, extremists, terrorists, subversive, political delinquent or ideological delinquent. Instead, and in pursuance of official regulations, the terms used should be: layabouts, criminals, delinquents, evil-livers, malefactors and other similar definitions contained in the Penal Code.

A qualitative leap forward

CC, arrested during the withdrawal from Pando and at present held at the Punta Carretas Penal Establishment, is a veteran of the National Liberation Movement although he is only 25 years old. As is the usual practice with the militants of the organisation he refused to allow his name to appear in this report. The watchword is 'No Sacred Cows'.

'What was the objective of the Pando operation?'

'To carry out an operation within the framework of an overall strategic plan aimed at achieving a qualitative leap forward.'

'Seeing that Pando was to be taken and then immediately relinquished, I wonder whether what you had in mind was to carry out a sort of experiment, or perhaps to make a show of strength?'

'Both.'

'Was the show of strength intended to impress your own side or the enemy?'

'It was intended to impress the public, the enemy, and us too. We were also pursuing minor objectives such as obtaining equipment, funds and publicity.'

'And offering a homage to Che . . .'

'Yes, by making the whole exploit into a homage to Che Guevara we intended – through the inevitable repercussions it was bound to have all over the South American continent – that the affair should carry an explicitly Latin American message.'

'You say that this operation was conceived within a framework of an overall plan aimed at achieving a qualitative leap forward. Was this particular operation to be the springboard for the whole leap?'

'No, the leap would be achieved through a series of larger or smaller operations – exploits – conforming to a general plan. Operation Pando was only a part of that general plan.'

'When did you resolve on the general plan?'

'End of '68, early '69.'

'Why did you feel the need for such a change – such a jump – just at that time?'

'There were changes in the internal context of the Movement itself, and in the country generally. The picture of repression – our enemy – was changing.'

'So in fact Pando was just one stage of a general plan?'

'You can see it was. In 1968 the NLM carried out four or five exploits which were widely publicised. There was the kidnapping of Pereyra Reverbel, and the raid on the Ariel Radio Station. There were two "expropriations" of explosives – and so on.'

'Did the main plan definitely encompass all the exploits which have so far been carried out?'

'In urban guerrilla warfare it isn't possible to draw up military-type tactical plans for the medium or long term. This is a very flexible form of warfare.'

'How many of the actions carried out in 1969 were the result of the new strategic plan?'

'Over 40. Under the plan there were five important operations in late 1968 and 40 in 1969.'

'The number of defeats sustained by your people also increased considerably. Up to late 1968 there were only about fifteen of you detained. How many are in detention today?'

'Right now – April 1970 – there are approximately 150 of us in prison, 128 men and 21 women.'

'How many of you are on the run – sought by the police?'

'In 1968 there were about 25. The police list is now thought to have over 100 on it.'

'How many dead?'

'Up to '68 three all told, one of them and two of us.'

'Flores and Robaina?'

'That's right. The total dead for both sides is now 17.'

'That means the change in revolutionary tactics has caused a parallel change in repressive tactics.'

'Yes, but don't forget it's a two-sided thing. They're at risk as well, and from our point of view even our defeats are exploits or battles or whatever – and have great publicity value. In his tricontinental message Che Guevara said "Publicity Vietcong style – what matters is the number of battles waged, never mind who wins."'

'Pando was then just one chapter in a general plan which does not outline actual exploits but only the general form these should take?'

'That's right.'

'All the same, there were special features which marked Pando out as quite different from any other exploit carried out within the same general framework – am I right?'

'There certainly was one obvious peculiarity which became apparent in the results, and that was that the operation, planned in line with a predetermined context, reacted on this context so as to necessitate the formulation of further plans to meet the new situation created.'

'Was the operation definitely a success?'

'In the sense of its place within the strategic framework it was a success. We effectively carried out the most important guerrilla action in recent times in Latin America. We seized a town. We mobilised over 100 men.'

'The newspapers said 40.'

'The police, we ourselves and anybody knowing anything of military matters must know that's a ridiculous figure. Of course we aren't only counting the active groups, but also those supporting. Anybody who has a concept of these things knows you have to take the latter into account – you include it in your plans, envisage it.'

'You say that strategically it was a success. In what sense, then, was it a failure?'

'In regard to the minor objectives – funds, equipment.'

'Within your general overall framework how would you evaluate the 3 dead, 16 taken prisoner, losses of arms and vehicles and the overrunning of your bases or hideouts by the other side?'

'These were undoubted blows and we suffered them as such, but they didn't detract from the fundamental objectives achieved by the operation which were: to demonstrate that there is a guerrilla movement capable of seizing a town, and to mount a homage to Che Guevara with its inevitable continental repercussions. Besides, those losses have not really weakened us in any way. The fact that we had not really sustained a serious setback was clearly demonstrated by the exploits which followed Pando without any obvious interruption. The organisation was, if anything, strengthened and its growth hastened. In this sense the operation was also successful. After all, the main aim of a guerrilla movement at this stage is to grow both in quantity and quality. And growth achieved during a bitter, difficult stage is particularly valuable. Those who join at such a time know full well what their fate may be. The rhythm of 1969 was maintained unfalteringly. Operation Pando was followed by a dozen important exploits. Just think – on 15 October, a very few days after Pando, we exposed the activities of Etcheverrigaray & Petcho, a firm dealing in illegal exchange transactions, operating at Calle Missiones in the Old City. On 26 November we carried off the books and accountancy records of the Banco Frances e Italiano after working for two and a half hours inside the bank.

'I heard of a certain Colonel who said "After the affair at Pando, I, as a military man, am in a position to state categorically that no place in Uruguay is safe."

'Zina Fernandez [Chief of Police in Montevideo] acknowledged to one of our members that the exploit missed complete success by a mere hairsbreadth, and that had it been entirely successful, by which he meant had we not lost any of our men, there would have had to have been a flood of resignations in high places. The enemy are well aware of the respect which the National Liberation Movement has earned as a revolutionary movement.'

'What about the public? How did they react?'

'I believe that for the very first time a large proportion of the public evaluated the potential of the guerrilla movement. From that aspect Operation Pando has done more than most exploits towards creating subjective conditions.'

'How do you evaluate the tactics employed to carry out the operation?'

'The action was faultless in regard to taking the town. From the subsequent police statements one can judge to what extent and how efficiently the town was brought under our control.'

'In that sense it was an important experiment for you all.'

'Yes – on the military plan very important. It was like an apprenticeship. It's not quite the same thing to hold up a bank as to take a town.'

'Did you get any support from the population?'

'Yes – there were numerous instances. One of our men was guarding the door of one of the banks with his gun in his hand. A window was thrown open and an old lady stuck her head out and asked, "What's going on?" Our man answered, "We're Tupamaros – we're expropriating funds." "Good," she said, "more power to your elbow," and closed the window. Later, during the withdrawal many of us were saved by the solidarity of the public.'

'Was Pando the first time you became aware of this support – sympathy – solidarity?'

'In Pando it just was much more obvious because the support was so massive. But we've felt the public to be on our side right through last year and during this year. There's a strange sort of rapport between the members of the NLM and the people they have supposedly overcome during these exploits – doormen, guards, nightwatchmen, owners of vehicles, and so on. There's a kind of silent dialogue between captor and captured which is difficult to understand for those who are not on the beam.'

'I can see that the taking of the town was a success from the tactical point of view. Why did the withdrawal break down, and how great, proportionately, was this breakdown?'

'The failure only affected a very small part of the contingent participating in the operation. Why there should have been any failure at all will take a little longer to explain. There were a number of unforeseen hitches which I'll explain as I go along.'

'Who decided in the first place that the taking of a town would be politically useful?'

'The leaders of the organisation.'

'And why was Pando chosen?'

'Well: from the moment we considered it would be politically useful to take a town we began to survey a number of towns. Pando seemed suitable because it is close to Montevideo, well populated, active, with a large and flourishing business and financial centre, and yet it's a small town. In the final analysis we also chose it because we had excellent tactical information about Pando.'

'When did you begin to prepare the operation?'

'Around 20 September.'

'That seems a very short preparation.'

'That part also was experimental.'

'What things do you have to take into account when you prepare an exploit like Operation Pando?'

'The first thing is to fill in the preliminary, sketchy information, putting in as much detail as possible. Once all such information has been accumulated we go on to laying our plans from five, basic points, which are:

1. The separate actions to make up the whole operation.
2. Coordination.
3. Arrival in the town.
4. Withdrawal from the town.
5. Logistic support (first aid, communications, base of operations, vehicles, publicity).

'As far as the actions themselves are concerned, once it's been decided which objectives are to be attacked, teams are formed and each team is allocated a definite objective. These teams, once picked, begin their own work of preparation, casing their particular objectives, so that further information is added to the pool of data already amassed. In planning an operation on the Pando scale one starts with one overall working plan or blueprint – but what happens? As you examine the details more thoroughly you find this first plan has to be modified. Then as each team works on its own particular objective, the new material they bring to the central pool frequently means further, and perhaps drastic, changes in the overall plan.

'For instance, a plan of action against objective A could conceivably interfere with a plan of action against objective B. Another important factor which could alter the original plan is time. This forces us to act within very strict time limits which are never ideal. If we were a regular army we could often handle problems arising with some degree of flexibility. But *we* always have to work against time. Everything has to be done in the shortest possible time.'

'This must be terribly important when coordinating all aspects of such an operation.'

'Coordination has to be streamlined to the nth degree. In the case of Pando we were going to be in action only 30 kilometres away from Montevideo, with fast, excellent highways available to the forces of repression.

'Moreover it was 8 October [the anniversary of Guevara's death] and the authorities would presume that you'd be up to something.'

'Exactly – they'd be on the lookout and we knew it. First problem then, how to reach Pando without arousing suspicion.'

'The funeral . . .'

'We didn't hit on that right away. It was a solution that occurred to us just a few days before the operation. We needed eleven vehicles. If we used any which had already been used on previous exploits they would be "branded" and would be dangerous. Then again, if each of the groups assigned to the various actions arrived a day or two beforehand, the repressive elements, authorities and so on would be alerted. If we used our own privately owned vehicles this would mean that for the future they would be "branded". We never use such vehicles if we can avoid it. The idea of the funeral came as a fantastic solution which did away with all the problems. Of course not all of us would arrive in the cortège, many would set off towards Pando from early morning onwards, using various forms of public transport. Those of us already in Pando would see that all was going well as we'd notice contingents of our members converging on certain points where they were supposed to converge.'

'How would you recognise them?'

'There was no one single person keeping a check on this part of the operation. Given our method of liaising between ourselves such a thing would have been impossible.'

'How would you be able to check then?'

'We'd better just ignore that – suffice it to say that there are various methods which are efficient, don't cancel each other out, and which are based on the principle of cutting down recognition between the militants to an absolute minimum.'

'You said that the first plan was modified as you went along – as each one of the definite objectives was planned. What about problems arising quite apart from the objectives themselves – for instance from the logistics angle?'

'The same applies. When you're coordinating first aid, publicity, bases of operations and many other things like that, you sketch out a preliminary plan and then alter it as you go along until you arrive at the final, definitive plan. Sometimes the definitive plan bears little relation to the original. In the case of Pando we had our definitive plan by Saturday, 4 October.'

'Give it to me briefly.'

'We were to go into action at 1300 hrs precisely – one o'clock. At that time all our systems would be go.'

'And was the signal to trigger action simply the time itself?'

'No – there was one person in charge of checking that all was in order. He would take care of unforeseen contingencies and would give the final signal to go.'

'How many separate objectives were there?'

'Six. The police station, the fire brigade next door, the telephone exchange and three banks. The police station – where the operation would start – was the key to the whole thing.'

'Did you have any major problems in occupying it?'

'No – it was completely overcome within the allotted time, but there was one incident which afterwards complicated our withdrawal.'

'I take it that the withdrawal was the most complex stage of the whole operation?'

'It certainly was the most difficult.'

'If the police station was overcome within the time planned, why did it upset your withdrawal?'

'Because – right then – at the very first stage, shots were exchanged. One of the policemen put up a fight. He was quickly overcome but somebody outside caught on that the police station was being attacked. If the police were out of action where would help be obtained in Pando? So he immediately decided to set off to get help in Montevideo, but he'd only gone about two kilometres along the road when he met the Highway Patrol who raised the alarm over the radio. This meant that the alarm had already been raised in Montevideo within four or five minutes of the start of Operation Pando.'

'Hadn't such a possibility been taken into account?'

'It wasn't a case of our not taking it into account. We'd thought about it all right, but we had to risk it. How on earth could we have guarded the whole periphery of Pando?'

'You say that the whole operation had to be completed within the shortest possible time. How long had you allowed?'

'That's where the second hitch comes in. The whole operation was to take a maximum of 15 minutes from start to finish. But it so happened that at the end of the attack on the Bank of Pando, just when the men were ready to leave the bank, a policeman suddenly appeared and esconced himself behind the getaway vehicle, from which point he covered the door of the bank with his gun. This had a twofold effect: we wasted precious minutes exchanging shots, and we lost subsequent use of one of the vehicles for the main withdrawal as this particular car was riddled with bullets and practically useless.

'It just managed to get the men back to the general meeting point where the cortège was waiting for them. Additionally, one of the mourners' cars developed a serious mechanical fault and had to be abandoned. This meant that the good cars had to be greatly overloaded and consequently, instead of keeping up a speed of 80 kilometres, they could only do 70. All the same, despite the time wasted and the promptness with which the police had been alerted – and I must remind you that they were notified almost simultaneously with the beginning of the action – despite all this they were unable to mount an effective counter-offensive. Most of our men got through the police cordon which was only just being organised. Only three cars, and those by a few short minutes, were caught in the trap at Toledo Chico. What the police certainly don't know is how many of our men got out of the trap itself, thanks to being given protection and shelter by the local people.'

An interview with a Tupamaro

It is not enough to be a rebel

I had first tried to interview him in November 1968. At that time he had been in prison for one month – the first of many months still to come. Although I had hardly expected to find him subdued and downcast, I had not expected to find him so whole. I had made up my mind on having the interview. I wanted to question him, to look for those signs which mark a man out as a revolutionary. But on that occasion I was the one who was interviewed and questioned. My questions were countered by other questions, my answers ruthlessly taken apart. The arguments I raised in an attempt to justify the interview and enable me to pursue it were knocked flat. It was an unequal contest – during which I was unable to take a single note. On the one side was a man who would not be convinced or shaken by jail or by the wiles of any journalist, however obstinate and determined; on the other side there was me, obstinate as hell and, I hope, determined, but caught in my own game, involving myself ever deeper in an irritating struggle with my own conscience.

When I next approached him summer had gone and we were well into autumn. He was still the same alive, cheerful and optimistic man I had seen on the previous occasion. The picture of an honest and dignified working man. Nothing had changed him during the intervening five months. For a second time I told him I would like to interview him. When I realised that he was not adamantly opposed to the idea I immediately set a pattern for our talk. 'Please,' I said, 'don't answer all my questions with questions of your own.' 'What are you afraid of?' he asked. 'I'm afraid that for a second time there may be no report.' 'Do you mean to tell me that you think your report more important than trying to understand?' 'There you go again,' I said 'Answering my questions with other questions.' He smiled. 'OK,' he said, 'but you must promise that my name won't appear at all.'

'Why not?'

'It wouldn't interest anybody. Names aren't important.'

'So when you talk you'll commit the whole organisation.'

'What if I do? You won't stop that by mentioning my name.

Some of the things I say would obviously commit the organisation, others won't. Go on – ask away.'

'Why did you refuse to let me interview you five months ago when now you don't mind?'

'A lot's happened in the five months.'

'That's true, a lot has happened. But how does this explain your willingness to talk now?'

'When I say a lot's happened maybe we're thinking of different things. I wouldn't know. I was referring to the two books which have come out on the organisation, and the reports which appeared in *Al rojo vivo**.'

'I see.'

'So you see the silence had already been broken. This report you're doing now could add points of view you couldn't expect to get from anybody outside our organisation.'

'What do you think Fidel meant when he said: "The fundamental thing in man is to be revolutionary"?'

'I think he meant that man's attitude to the world should be one of constant renewal.'

'So you don't think his words are limited to the political sphere?'

'Definitely not. I think that "revolutionary" has to be taken in a much fuller sense.'

'So the essential thing in man would be . . .'

'. . . The most important thing in man is to transform the world in which he lives by his actions and his thoughts – without any sort of limitation. There is revolutionary painting, and reactionary painting, because there are revolutionary painters and reactionary painters.'

'Do you consider yourself to be a revolutionary in this all-embracing sense in which we are talking?'

'It's difficult to say this about oneself. Let's say I try to be.'

'Would you say this applied to every sphere? You talk about painting. Would you apply it to art in general?'

'Yes, of course. I can't conceive of art which isn't free . . . but if we get on this subject we'll go on for ever.'

'If I were to ask you why you are a revolutionary?'

'I would prefer that you ask me why a man becomes a revolutionary. I don't believe men are born revolutionaries – they're made

* *Al rojo vivo*, broadly translated as *Red in Tooth and Claw*, a weekly paper specialising in crime reports.

135

that way. If we scratch a revolutionary we find a rebel underneath. But it isn't enough to be a rebel.'

'It's a good start.'

'Yes – but only a start. To take the step from being a rebel to being a revolutionary you have to do a great deal of soul searching, you've got to become aware. If you don't know exactly what you're doing one could end, in the best of circumstances, as a Pancho Villa, a magnificent rebel, but a man who without revolutionary training could easily turn into a tool of the counter-revolution.'

'Don't you think a lot of it is a wish for adventure, for personal achievement. Don't you think there's a lot of that in the attitude of the revolutionary?'

'I don't think you'd have had the idea without a certain seeking after adventure. Perhaps at the start we were all a bit adventurous.'

'Are you referring to the founders of the NLM? Tell me about those early days.'

'We were a tiny handful of enthusiasts.'

'What did you set out to do? What were you seeking?'

'We knew there were two or three things we wanted. But if you think we had even a notion of where it would all lead to, that what we are doing today would be possible, you're wrong, we didn't. We had a general idea and a lot of faith. It has been said that we arose as a consequence of the failure of the UP [the period of rule by plural executive, and no president, 1952–1967].'

'Wasn't that the beginning?'

'No – the beginning was earlier. In a way it was born in the Socialist Party but before the famous breakdown. I would place it at the time when we were starting to fight against the Frugoni line: that fight was the result of nonconformism engendered by the lack of revolutionary push in the Party. Of course at that time we had no idea at all that the fight would become a battle with arms.'

'When did you first get the idea of using arms?'

'At the time when Fusco's security measures were being instituted. That was the time when we had actual evidence of the ineffectualness of the existing parties and the unions to meet a situation of that sort.'

'You told me that at that time there were two or three things which were very clear.'

'Yes: we knew for instance that the existing parties, in their manner of operating, were ineffectual in achieving the solutions that they themselves proposed.'

'They were useless? Had they ever been useful?'

'No – not very much. They had served their purpose in one important aspect . . .'

'You're referring of course to the Socialist and Communist parties . . .'

'Yes, they had made quite large sections of the population politically minded, and these sections would be the natural source of supply for the revolutionary movement. We knew all that, but we also knew at that stage, something else.'

'Which was?'

'That rather than knowing clearly what we *had* to do, we knew what we ought not to do.'

'And what was that?'

'To affirm our political personality by attacking other leftist groups. We knew all about the sterility of these leftist squabbles, we felt they should stop. We all had to work positively. Once we had established what our line was, the sounder elements joined us. It wasn't a case of declaring that our line was the only valid line to follow. Whether it was the only line or not was something to be proved by the facts.'

'Do you consider that polemics – talking – between the various sectors on the Left is quite useless?'

'Let's talk about something real, not theories. If you could have really objective and constructive discussions I wouldn't think these useless but what happens to these discussions in practice? Each sector is wedded to its own particular "truth" and isn't going to give it up no matter what. There's no use in talking like that, I don't have to explain why such discussions are useless.'

'The initiators of the Movement sprung from a common origin then? The Socialist Party . . .'

'Not all of us, some of us had belonged to the Socialist Party, but taken as a whole we were a real hotch-potch, a sort of mosaic of ideologies.'

'United solely by one common idea in regard to the inefficiency of the established parties?'

'Not solely . . .'

'And by the conviction that a party cannot consolidate its personality on the basis of the mistakes of the other parties?'

'That still wasn't the whole of it. We were soon united by something more positive, the will to create an apparatus that would fight with arms.'

'If you put it like that it sounds as if armed fighting was an end in itself.'

'I've already told you we were all from the Left.'

'Do you mean by this to tell me that there was clear agreement on the final objective?'

'Surely – the final objective was socialism. Well, we hadn't gone very far before we realised that an apparatus which is going to fight with arms needs a firm discipline, but not one imposed from outside. It has to be the conscious self-discipline of the individual who knows what he's fighting for and is pursuing clear objectives. As I told you, we were made up like an ideological mosaic. Each one of us, to a lesser or greater degree, was tied by an umbilical cord to the original movement from which he had sprung. This mosaic had to be shattered. We couldn't achieve our aims unless we had a coherent, integrated ideology.'

'And your agreement on the final objective and on the need to fight with arms was not sufficient to produce this cohesion?'

'No. We were pretty clear about the need to fight with arms but we only achieved real coherence when we reached an agreement on the method we would adopt, special aspects of the method, when it became evident that all other forms of fighting would have to be subjective to it.'

'Subjective to armed fighting? Surely you mean substituted by it?'

'Not at all. The work with the masses for instance, both from the political and the trade-union angle, continued to be fundamental. But for us this work had to lead to the training of a large contingent which could be drawn on for the armed fight. That's why I used the word subjective. The supreme effort would be the armed fight, and this would unite and coordinate behind it all other forms of struggle.'

'What were for you the more obvious or important objectives for direct action?'

'They were, and still are, to act against the régime, to publicise our political line and to train our men.'

'When you'd arrived at that stage did you prepare a programme?'

He smiled. 'Come what may, you are determined to see our

future neatly tabulated on a page, marked item 1, item 2 and so on. OK. If you must. We drew up a programme. Nothing long-term. No bombastic strategic or tactical plans. Nothing like that. I think one of our greatest virtues early on was that we tried to stick to reality. We only undertook what was within our scope and our means. We knew the working class was our natural source of man-power supply but to think we could call on any man at random when we were ourselves a mere half dozen would have been illusory. We had to wait for men to prove themselves in their own milieu.'

'You mean union militants who would ideologically be close to you?'

'Yes – when men like that were thrown up that would be the time to plan the work to be done. It's no good planning work unless you've got somebody to do it.'

'I've often wondered whether you were active within the unions and, if so, how you managed it, given the nature of your organisation.'

'Most of us have personal contacts. It's easy to know who is well thought of in the union – they stand out.'

'And from your point of view those with the most radical views would be the most suitable?'

'In general, yes, but by itself this wouldn't be enough. A man must also have a clear vision of the ultimate aims of the trade-union movement, realise that these are not merely to resolve immediate economic problems but rather to transform the conditions under which workers are exploited.'

'So . . .'

'Wait – there's more to come. He must also be convinced that these conditions can only be finally and definitely changed by means of revolutionary struggle aimed at taking power.'

'In that case the term "radical" seems inadequate.'

'It was your word, not mine.'

'Touché. So in fact you seek contacts with people with broadly similar ideological views to the NLM?'

'Yes – we never waste our efforts trying to start from dead cold. Besides, it's often very difficult for people with years of trade-union militancy behind them to establish a theoretical or practical relation between their work and ours.'

'I would have thought it would have been quite the reverse.'

'Well, of course we've gone part of the way along the same road.' We've something in common with a man who has had experience of union struggles but there's a gulf between us. Our trade unionist has got used to fighting for economic goals and, without realising it, he's made these his ultimate aim. Now we think differently. We believe that improvements in wages and similar goals are simply means to an end. A way of uniting the workers. From then on the fight has to be waged along its true lines. As the demands become ever more radical there's bound to come a time when the workers wake up to the fact that their movement as it is structured cannot possibly stand up to the violence which the Government will unleash, and that moreover unions can only function efficiently within the law. When this stage is reached union action becomes the precursor to political action.'

'In reply to one of the "Thirty Points"* it was said that conditions governing your strategy were the crisis situation, the high degree of unionisation of the workers, the degree of preparation of the armed revolutionary group and so on. Would you say that those same circumstances would be basic to your strategy today or have things changed in the past two years?'

'As far as the crisis, that's still going on, as we know, and is now much more serious than it was then, and is much worse than is apparent. Things are happening at such a speed. Uruguay can no longer escape from the circumstances which are engulfing the rest of America. We used to be a sort of island, but not any more, we're just falling in with the general Latin American pattern.'

'What about the unions? Wouldn't you say they've had some serious setbacks during the past year?'

'Yes, to some extent. But you've got to have these to make you understand that there's a need to change organisational schemes and methods of fighting.'

'Do you think the experience of the past two years justifies to some extent the choice of the city as the setting for guerrilla warfare?'

'Indeed I think it has confirmed that this is the proper way to fight.'

'How do you explain the loss of so many men recently?'

* Thirty Points: the manifesto of the Broad Front, the political party supported by the Tupamaros.

'I should think that would be obvious. When an organisation like ours grows – and ours is growing rapidly – security mechanisms are strained. There is insufficient time to train new cadres. There's another thing too. The same men who catch our eye because we consider them potential militants have also caught the eye of the police for the same reason.'

'You think the movement is growing rapidly? Does this indicate that the subjective conditions of our country have changed?'

'Yes, it certainly is an indication. What you call subjective conditions – not a term I much like – have indeed changed. The means of cushioning the public from reality have broken down. People are rapidly becoming aware of the real situation. The incurable crisis . . . government corruption . . .'

'Do you think the NLM has a part to play in this phenomenon of dawning public awareness?'

'We've contributed. Don't you think our exploit against Financiera Monty which disclosed all sorts of transactions implicating government personalities was important? Anyway we mustn't forget that government action has favoured us enormously.'

'What do you think the general feeling is in regard to your Movement and its fighting methods?'

'I would say that people are beginning to understand what we're trying to do, in the sense that there can be no solution without armed combat. But I think we've still got to spell it out to the individual. We've created a great feeling of expectancy and an avid curiosity about who we are and where we're going. It's up to us now to show that we have a clear concept of how a revolutionary fight is waged.'

'You have several years of experience as a member of the NLM. Were you one of the founders?'

'Yes.'

'I would be very interested to know whether at any time you noticed in yourself or in any of your friends signs of the serious psychological consequences which Debray foresaw for the urban guerrilla?'

'Do you mean what the Frenchman called "split personality"?'

'That's right. The awful dissociation which the urban guerrilla must suffer because he has to live two quite separate lives: one apparently quite normal, and underneath the other, clandestine existence.'

'We've seen no sign of it so far. Anyway, even if it does produce split personalities, there's no other way except by fighting and we must press on. I don't suppose the younger generations of Vietnamese know anything else except killing. It's their way of life. Don't you think that must create serious traumas in a human being. Psychological problems of the worst sort? Have you read Fanon?'

'*The Condemned of the Earth* – yes.'

'Well, you tell me – even if Debray's predictions were true, what alternative have we got?'

'What about what Debray calls "war neurosis" which he says is inevitable in the urban guerrilla?'

'There's no proof – no proof at all.'

My interviewee spoke with the calm assurance of one conjuring away all possible neuroses or even the very idea of such. He went on: 'You must read the *Newspaper*. What do you suppose the "shut-in look" that Che talks about is?'

'What do you think is the most difficult time for a militant? Most difficult because he feels unable to cope?'

He scratched his head, looked at me and then looked at his hands. 'I don't know why I don't immediately shout "when he's being tortured".'

Then he said, quite quietly, 'You want to know from my own experience?'

'You were tortured?'

'Yes – it's a pretty experience, I can tell you.'

'I've never seen anybody put on such a polished appearance of unconcern. You can't feel as casual as all that about it.'

'Wait a moment, we have to get things straight. It is an extremely difficult moment to live through, but it helps one. Helps one to know oneself. To know the value one places on existence. I'll tell you something which is worse – to see a friend fall and not be able to help him. I don't know how I'd feel.'

'Would you say you are less able to cope with not being able to help a friend than with your own pain?'

'I don't know – it hasn't happened to me, but I think it must be one of the hardest things to bear.'

'When somebody asks to join the movement I suppose he must feel an ideological and moral affinity with its aims. But despite this I presume that the organisation would have to encourage certain traits and discourage others. In other words you'd have to try to make this man into a useful militant.'

'One thing is basic – a revolution has to take men as they come. We can't create them in our image. Those of us who have been in the Movement for years still falter at times. You mustn't forget the precepts we sucked in with our mother's milk. All the same we do try to work on the new member. We call it proletarising him.'

'What does that consist of?'

'It consists of fostering in him a spirit of comradeship and an awareness of self-discipline.'

'Why do you call it proletarisation?'

'Let me finish . . . the most important thing is to create in him a feeling of dependence on the group. He has to be aware of the fact that he cannot be self-sufficient – that the others are essential to him. It's called "proletarisation" because that is the proper feeling for a worker. The methods of production in a capitalist régime develop an awareness of the relationship with other workers. The worker knows that what he produces is not the result of his own efforts alone but the result of collective effort.'

'And that isn't a feeling which applies to the petit bourgeois?'

'The petit bourgeois feels himself to be self-sufficient. Another thing we have to make the newcomer to the movement understand – and this is generally very difficult – is that the revolution goes forward by dint of small and continual effort, that the heroic episode is over in a flash, and that the tedious, apparently unnoticed and unimportant activities make up the bulk of the work. Once a militant understands this he has perhaps understood the essence.'

'What character trait would you say was most important for a Tupamaro?'

'That he should be willing and – do you remember what Che said about honesty?'

'Yes. "You can make a revolutionary out of an honest man."'

'Exactly – if a man is willing and honest, you can make a revolutionary out of him.'

143

Tortures

To appreciate the degree of fear felt by a system when forces within begin to tear it apart, one has only to examine the means used by the apparatus set up to defend itself.

The interviews reported below speak of this fear.

I

Eleuterio Fernandez Hidobro was arrested at Toledo Chico on 8 October 1969, during the withdrawal from Pando.

'They caught me at the Abrevadero and Andaluz intersection. I was caught by a picket of the Metropolitan Guard. They're known as shock troops – the A1 Guard – under the command of a man called Pecho or Petcho. I'm not sure how it's spelt. They caught me and disarmed me, and then set about beating me with the butts of their guns and kicking me.'

'How many were they?'

'I don't know – 12 or 15. As soon as they caught me they started to beat me up. They didn't even ask my name. Some who were some way off came running to join in.'

'The officer in charge too?'

'No – he kept shouting at them to leave me alone but they only half obeyed and then started up again. I got the feeling he couldn't control them. He had to shout so much. He kept telling them that I had to be in one piece for the interrogation but they wouldn't listen. They were in a right state of disorder, firing in the air to attract each other's attention and firing at my feet although I hadn't moved a finger. They kept insulting me and shoving me around and daring me to run away.'

'To run away?'

'Yes they'd say, "Go on – run, so we can fill you with lead."'

'And what did you do?'

'What d'you think? I knew they weren't joking.'

'How did they know when they caught you that you'd been involved in the Pando affair?'

'They could tell because I was covered with mud and my clothes were torn. Besides even if I hadn't been in such a state, they'd probably still have taken me – they arrested a lot of people who were completely innocent and had had nothing to do with the taking of Pando, and they treated them just the same. Beating and pushing them around until they got to the prison van and then more beatings to get them to get in.'

'What happened afterwards?'

'The officer finally managed to control them and whilst he was actually with me they left me alone. But he had to go away and talk over the radio – as soon as he turned his back they started up again, they beat me, spat on me, the lot. The odd thing is that the officer was just as angry as they were, but I think he simply had a different sort of mentality.'

'Were you in a lonely place? Couldn't anybody have intervened, helped you?'

'Some local people tried to approach but they were warned to go back to their homes.'

'How long did this go on?'

'For a while. I don't know exactly. They kept on saying, "Why didn't we kill you right away?" "Why don't you try to beat it?" And so on. But I'll tell you one thing – I got something positive out of all this.'

'How do you mean?'

'Well – I learnt something I didn't know before. The experience of those few hours showed me that sadism, torture and murder are not necessarily carried out on instructions from above. I realised that all levels were corrupted, and pretty thoroughly so that the men couldn't be controlled. I could hear them complaining that there were so few deaths. Every time the loudspeaker mentioned the number of dead they would complain bitterly. "So few," they'd say. "It should be more." "What? – only three . . ." And then later, in the prison van . . .'

'What happened?'

'The officer was sitting in front with the driver. When he got in he told the men to leave me alone, not to be smart . . . but as soon as the van started on its way, the man alongside me began to pick at the wounds on my head.'

'To pick? What do you mean?'

'He would force them open and make them bleed and get his fingers full of blood and then wipe them on my clothes.'

'What on earth did the others say?'

'They laughed. When he got tired of that game he started to play with his revolver. He'd put it to my temple and spin the drum and press the trigger. The others warned him then that he'd kill me. So he stopped that and started on a new tack – telling me what they were going to do to me and to my wife.'

'What sort of things? Obscene things?'

'Yes – obscenities.'

'What happened when you arrived at Police Headquarters?'

'Nothing special – they treated me like they do everybody. There were uniformed men from all the districts, and plain-clothes men and they all beat me – they seemed to be in a blind fury. Even the dwarf from Central Prison, who is an administrator, joined in.'

'What happened afterwards?'

'The usual – I don't want to mention it.'

'No, I mean before that, before they transferred you to the prison van.'

'They made us kneel behind the van, facing the inside.'

'"Us" – who else was there?'

'Another of our members – a chap called Puig. I realised then that the officer had recognised me from the very start. He knew that I had been on the run for some time.'

'How did you realise this?'

'By the way he spoke. He came up to me and said, "Lad – you're thinner."'

'Did he say anything else?'

'Yes – he asked me what had been our intentions at Pando, and then he went on to ask about other things – he was interested in the political side.'

'Did you answer him – could you actually talk to him?'

'Yes.'

'Did you talk for long?'

'No – several top brass arrived almost immediately.'

'Police?'

'I'm not sure – I suspect a lot of them were Army. The uniform wasn't like most of the police uniforms I know. They could have been from the Metropolitan Police and they could have been from the Army. I couldn't say one way or the other.'

'How did they come – in a car?'

'Walking, surrounded by men with their arms at the ready – they seemed worked up. When they appeared there was a deadly hush.

They took Petcho round to the front of the prison van. Although I couldn't see them I knew they were having a violent argument.'

'What did they say?'

'I listened hard but I only heard confused bits because the prison van radio, which was between them and me, was bleating-out orders. I did hear though quite clearly Petcho's parting shot which I think closed the discussion. He said, "I'm a Service man, I'm not a murderer."'

'What did the others say?'

'I couldn't hear anything they were saying, they were talking too quietly. Petcho came round to where I was and, spitting in my face, he said, "I've saved your life."'

II

Arapey Cabrera was arrested at Toledo Chico on 8 October 1969, during the withdrawal from Pando.

'Who arrested you?'

'Everybody. The Highway Patrol, men from the Metropolitan Guard, Army men, the lot. When I opened my eyes I could see hundreds of boots around my head. It was like a nightmare, a sea of boots swirling about. I couldn't really make out anything else. I couldn't see their faces or uniforms or anything.'

'I heard that they started to torture you right there.'

'Torture? I'd just call it ill treatment – though perhaps that's not expressive enough. I don't know – call it attrition perhaps. They started to wear me down.'

'OK. We'll call it attrition if you like. You could see boots all round you? You were down on the ground?'

'That's right – face down, semi-conscious with one arm shot to pieces.'

'And what did they do to you?'

'They started to question me, beating and kicking me at the same time. They kicked my legs and my head. I could hardly hear what they were asking. I know at one point somebody thrust an identity card in my face and said, "This isn't you – Who the hell are you?" I couldn't really think straight, but I did manage to say that the identity card was mine.'

'And was it?'

'Yes.'

'Why wouldn't they believe you?'

'Well – it was an old identity card. I'd taken it out for my matric, it must have been ten years old. I must admit I looked like a kid in the photograph.'

'Did you manage to convince them it was you?'

'I don't know – anyway it didn't really matter. They kicked me just the same and trod on my wounded arm. Then somebody called out, "Watch it – there's a journalist," and somebody else said "Keep him away – we don't want him nosing around here." Right away they made a tight little wall of policemen round me.'

'Why would they want to hide you?'

'I don't know. They kept putting my name out over the radio. Said I was wounded. I don't know why they'd want to hide me. You'd have to ask them.'

'How long did you lie there bleeding?'

'I don't know exactly. They'd shot me about two o'clock and they took me to hospital around four.'

'Why did they take so long?'

'That's something else you'd have to ask them.'

'Were they hoping you'd bleed to death or something?'

'I suppose so – and if they'd left me much longer I would have.'

'Then what happened?'

'At one stage – I'm not sure exactly when – they started to harp on the Pellegrini thing, asking where he was and who would know where to find him.'

'What did you say?'

'I didn't know and I told them I didn't know. Then they put their lighted cigarettes to my arm.'

'Your wounded arm?'

'Yes.'

'Did they burn you on the wound?'

'Right by the wound.'

'And you're telling me they didn't torture you.'

'Well – I couldn't really feel anything, I was practically dying by then.'

'Did you know you were dying?'

'I didn't then but later I did. I realised I must have been in what's called the "rosy death" phase.'

'What's that? Why rosy?'

'I'm not sure, it could be because of the pink colour of the water when somebody cuts their wrists and bleeds to death in the bath. Or maybe it's something to do with the progressive anaemia, you get paler and pinker as your life blood seeps away.'

'Didn't you feel any anguish?'

'No – none at all. I drifted in and out of consciousness several times – quite peacefully.'

'At such a time – does one think of death?'

'I couldn't say that one doesn't think of death. Well, at least I couldn't say that I personally didn't think of death – I did, but death at that moment seemed of secondary importance. It didn't worry me. It was really very odd. I felt as if I'd been left behind by events and things – or that I was somehow at their mercy, enslaved by them.'

'I can understand your being left behind. That can happen at any time – you feel uninvolved in regard to events which affect you. But how could you be at their mercy? Why?'

'Because I had expected to meet a situation which would be perfectly familiar, and the situation that I had to face in the event was nothing like what I had foreseen. That's why I say I was at the mercy of events and things – I was disorientated.'

'Was this feeling to do with death or with the way the police handled things.'

'No, much bigger, more fundamental. It could be summarised in just one word – war. I really lived a war situation then. Several things contributed to produce this experience. The behaviour of the police, my own closeness to death and – above all – seeing one of our members killed.'

'Salerno?'

'Yes – Salerno.'

'Were you with him when he fell?'

'Yes – we were together.'

'Begin at the beginning.'

'Well – we were running along just by the road, near some wire fencing. Salerno was armed and he ran towards a little eucalyptus wood on a slight rise and shouted to me to follow. I did, and that was when I got my first shot in the arm. The shooting went on but Salerno was soon out of ammunition and he asked me what we should do. I said I was shot in the arm and we should surrender. He agreed and we got ready to go out and give ourselves up.'

'What about the school?'

'What school?'

'When did you go into the school?'

'I don't know. There was a school opposite.'

'But listen – I mean the school mentioned in the newspapers.'

'I don't know – I don't know what the papers said. I didn't see them. I don't know anything about the school. I know one of our girls took cover in the school. We were never in the school.'

'So you decided it was better to give yourselves up?'

'That's right. We decided to surrender. Salerno came out from behind the tree where he was sheltering and, so that the police would know we were surrendering, he threw his gun down straight away – a big Luger or Mauser it was – and at the same time he shouted that we were surrendering and put his arms up above his head.'

'Did he call out "We surrender"?'

'Yes – he called out, "We surrender – we give in," and he started to walk slowly, ever so slowly, with his arms above his head. I watched him go. He'd gone about three metres when a burst of firing from the right brought him down. There were ten bullets in his body.'

'Had you been friends long?'

'I'd only just met him – a few minutes earlier. We'd just exchanged a few words. For him they were his last. He didn't know who I was and I didn't know who he was. We were two poor bloody soldiers doing what we could for the cause.'

III

Jesus David Melian was arrested at Toledo Chico on 8 October 1969, during the withdrawal from Pando.

'I was arrested by the Highway Police.'

'Were there many?'

'Two of us, Elbio Cardozo and me.'

'I meant the police. Were there many of them?'

'Three, the officer in charge and two others.'

'Did they search you?'

'Yes. They searched us, asked our names and then made us lie face down by the roadside.'

'Did they treat you properly?'

'Oh, yes. We'd been lying there for a little while when some police from the Metro appeared. They told the Highway Patrol they'd come to fetch us. Said they would take over. The patrolmen told them that they had arrested us and they would take us along themselves. I can still remember his voice as he said that.'

'Why do you remember his voice?'

'I'm not sure. It was quiet, but it was trembling a bit. I'd say he didn't like being asked to give us up.'

'Did the men from the Metro accept the patrolman's refusal?'

'No – an argument started. The patrolman kept his temper but I could tell he wasn't going to give way. The argument got really fierce. I thought they'd come to blows.'

'What reasons did the Metro man give for wanting to take you?'

'None – he was mad, like a wild beast who sees its prey getting away.'

'What about the patrolman?'

'I couldn't see him but at one point I thought he was at the end of his patience.'

'You mean he was going to give in?'

'No, I thought he'd punch the other fellow. Finally the Metro man, who must have been a corporal or a sergeant, realised the patrolman wasn't going to give in so he stopped arguing and came round to where we were lying and pressed his gun against my head.'

'A revolver?'

'No, bigger, maybe a machine-gun. I'm not sure. I was face down and could only see the end of the barrel. "We'll put a hole through this one's head right away," he said. The patrolman shouted something and grabbed him.'

'By the arm holding the gun?'

'The Metro man was holding the gun in both hands. I could just see as he was dragged off. The patrolman told him to get back and finally he did, but first he kicked me and then my friend on the head.'

'Do you think he would have fired?'

'I think he might have – he was so worked up. I'm not exaggerating. He really was in a state. If he and his men had been allowed to take us away I'm sure they'd have killed us. It's funny about the Metro police. There's something special about them. They seem chock-full of a blind hatred. They don't seem rational.'

'Do they come from the interior like most of the Army and Police?'

'Yes – they're usually out-of-work country people – green as anything. It would be interesting to find out how they train them so's to make them what they are.'

'What happened after they'd gone away?'

'The Highway Patrol made us get in their car and took us to 27 Division where we were transferred to a prison van and taken to Police Headquarters. That was when things really started to get bad.'

'Worse than the episode you've just been telling me about, when you thought you'd be shot at any moment?'

'What I've just told you looks impressive from a distance. At the time I didn't somehow seem to mind dying. It didn't seem so frightening. But Police Headquarters was a horrific nightmare. When we got there the van was driven in at basement level and, before opening the doors, two rows of police lined themselves up on either side between the van and the lift.'

'How far was that?'

'Ten metres – about. We had to run the gauntlet, except that we couldn't run. They made us go dreadfully slowly, and all the while we were being kicked and punched and beaten. The men shouted insults at us and some howled like wolves. I felt I was going through a tunnel and that I'd die before I got to the end. Everybody tried to get in as many blows as possible, never mind where they landed.'

'Where was the officer who'd taken you there?'

'That was Fontana. When we got down from the van he got down first and he purposefully walked very, very slowly so that his friends could really have their fun. Once he stopped, turned and said ironically, "You mustn't treat them like that, leave them alone, they're my prisoners . . ." When we got to the lift those who hadn't been able to line up at the sides came round in front of us and stopped us getting into the lift. Everybody wanted to go on hitting us. I felt as if I'd fallen into a snake pit. The lift gate seemed like the door out of hell. How wrong I was. The lift filled up with police who went on beating us. I got such a wallop on my right eye I thought I'd lost it. I could feel somebody down on the floor under my feet but couldn't tell if it was a friend or one of the police, anyway I couldn't do anything. I'd have had as much chance of doing something of my own accord as if I were being trampled by a herd of stampeding rhinoceroses. One man told me afterwards he thought the police were "high".

'You may think this funny but a lot of them were crying. The police I mean. I think it was mass hysteria. The lift finally stopped at the fourth floor and we got out. Osano was lying across the floor in a pool of blood. He couldn't get up because of the wound in his leg. He just lay there bleeding, with his hands tied.'

'Why did they take you to the fourth floor?'

'For Fontana to interrogate us. It was short and not sweet and ended with a threat. "OK," he said, "you needn't talk now if you don't want to. We'll make you talk – there's plenty of time."

'They took me back to the lift. Whilst we waited for it to come up they punched me on the back of the neck and in the kidneys. I tried to keep up by holding onto the grill but they finally pushed me down and began to jump on me. I bled all over the place. "We'll have to take him down the stairs," said one. "He'll muck up the lift with all that blood." "What's the odds," said another. "The lift's filthy already." When I got into the lift I passed out for a minute but recovered. When I got out of the lift there were two men waiting for me on either side of the lift gate and they started to punch me over the head and on the neck and face.'

'Were they from Investigaciones [CID]?'

'No, they were men from the Metro.'

'Did you get the feeling that permission to beat up the prisoners was a kind of "reward" for duties well done?'

'Yes – that's exactly how it was. Even administrative officers came to hit us.'

'What happened then?'

'They took me to a cell. There were two men from the Theft Squad there. One was short and greyhaired, and the other, I realised, was a southpaw. They made me turn with my face to the wall. I shut my eyes and tried to draw my head down, waiting for the blows. I waited. Then they put their hands in my trouser pockets and took 700 pesos which I never saw again.'

IV

Juan Antonio Ciola was very thin and very young, with a dark skin and a sad smile. Because of his dark skin I asked whether he was of Arab descent.

'No – my parents were from Southern Italy.'

'When were you arrested?'

'On 27 November last year, at Pinar.'

'Where did they take you?'

'To the police station at Shangrila.'

'Who took you there.'

'The police deputy chief. On the way he told me not to worry.'

'Were you nervous?'

'More or less – but he didn't say it because of that. He just said I wasn't to worry, we were going to have a friendly chat.'

'Did that relieve your mind?'

'No – I thought he was taking the mickey out of me.'

'What happened afterwards?'

'When we got down from the car he said he liked me, that he found me "simpatico" and he would recommend his men to give me special treatment.'

'And did they?'

'Yes – I'll say – very special. When we arrived he told his men "This is a friend of mine – you've got to give him a friend's treatment." Then they took me to a cell and one of Fontana's men started to question me.'

'And what did you do?'

'I didn't answer anything – so they started to beat me up.'

'Much?'

'Yes – quite a bit – I lost consciousness.'

'What did they hit you with?'

'Their fists – in the stomach.'

'They must have punched you a lot for you to faint.'

'Quite a lot – one held me and the other punched.'

'Were you handcuffed?'

'Yes – with my hands behind my back.'

'What happened when you came to?'

'I was in a water tank.'

'Why did they put you in there?'

'They said it was to stop me fainting. They said after I'd swallowed some water I wouldn't be so keen to faint, I'd behave better.'

'And did you?'

'Did I what?'

'Did you start to tell them what they wanted to know?'

'No.'

'How long did they keep you in the water?'

'Ten minutes. They kept pushing my head under and pulling it out again. Each time I swallowed more water. Finally I couldn't hear what they were asking. Then they took me out and started to burn my arms with their cigarettes. You can see the marks of the burns.' He rolled up his shirtsleeves to show me two red circles on each wrist.

'That must have been terribly painful.'

'I don't know, I was past caring. I couldn't hear or see, I collapsed like a rag doll. They'd drag me up and go on beating me. Finally they obviously hit me very hard on the head.'

'Why do you say "obviously"?'

'Because I didn't know anything about it. I woke up in the Military Hospital. An orderly said I had been there for 24 hours, My head ached like mad. I felt it and I realised I was all bandaged. I asked the orderly what had happened to me and he looked at me as if I was crazy. "Don't you know you've got a bloody great gash in your head?" he asked me. And that's how I found out.'

V

Lionel Martinez Platero was arrested on 8 October 1969. This interview took place a few days afterwards when he still bore the marks of the electric shocks on his body. It wasn't easy to make him talk. He had a grudge against the Press and all journalists. I kept his replies but not my questions.

'They put me in a police van to take me to the police station. During the journey they keep hitting and kicking me until we arrived at "Intelligence", where Otero questioned me for about three minutes. He told me that if I wouldn't talk he wouldn't be responsible for what was coming to me. I was then taken to a cell. They put a guard in with me – a huge man, well above normal height – maybe they were afraid I'd commit suicide if they left me alone. I threw myself on the floor and tried to sleep.

'But right away I heard steps in the corridor. The guard heard them too and knew what they meant. He told me to stand up and face the wall. Two or three men came in and one of them put a hood over my head. A sort of Ku Klux Klan thing with a hole in the top and a drawstring round the bottom. They took me out and turned me round several times. I thought they wanted to make me giddy. Then, somewhere around there, I couldn't be sure exactly where, they took all my clothes off and threw me down on a wet mattress supported on a sort of iron grid. The grid must have been slightly triangular in shape because although they opened my legs wide these were still supported from underneath. Then they strapped down my wrists and ankles and threw a bucket of cold water over me and then covered me with wet rags. Then they put a record on a record-player and turned it up full blast. It was a pop record. Then they threw questions at me and jabbed me with electric shocks alternately. Each time they gave me a shock the sods standing around clapped their hands in time to the music and yelled "twist – twist – twist". What with the music, the clapping and the yelling of the sods the noise was hellish. When I could think at all I kept thinking I must try to keep up my strength to resist – resist.

'They kept it up for twenty minutes, over and over, first questions, then shock, then insults. "You're going to be castrated." "We're going to scrape you out." "You won't be able to stand it." "You'd better talk or we'll hand you over to the soldiers." When they realised it was no use, that I was half unconscious and couldn't hear their questions, they dragged me off back to the cell and flung me down on the filth, the shit and piss on the floor. "We'll be back in a minute," they said.

'I knew I mustn't think of their coming back. I'd have to will myself to rest, to sleep so as to get my strength back.

'I'd just started to drop off when a Spaniard in the cell opposite started to scream like a maniac. He'd been "gone over" and was protesting with everything he knew, kicking and beating on the

door, screaming, "Torturers – show your faces. I've got balls.*
Murderers."

'On the floor above, the prostitutes who had heard the Spaniard,
as I had, chanted in chorus, "Torturers, murderers." Somebody
near my cell had a fit of the screaming abdabs. I presume it was
the photographer they had arrested by mistake. Inwardly cursing
the Spaniard and everybody who screamed I finally fell into a half-
sleep which rested me a bit.

'Soon – I don't know if it was one hour, two hours or only half
an hour – I heard the voices in the corridor again and recognised
the torturers. The footsteps stopped outside my cell. It was all
repeated just as before, except that this time they were angrier,
more aggressive. They threw a hessian sack, soaking wet, on me.
This made the electric shock worse. I began to tell lies. I told them
that I had been in Shangrila, had lived in a certain house in
Shangrila. Great activity, great expectations, we all went to
Shangrila. They surrounded the house I had mentioned and,
armed to the teeth, hammered on the door. Two very old people,
the picture of innocence, opened the door. They realised they had
been tricked. Infuriated they pushed me down to the beach and
made me kneel in the water. They told me they were going to
drown me.

'After a while they got tired of that and we got back into the van.
Beto and one other were in the van. It was our van. The one they
had confiscated when they arrested us. That was the last time I saw
it. We went out on the road and one of them said, "Now where?"
"To San José and Yi, we'll get through directly to the authorities,"
replied the other. It was dawn. They took me back to the cell and
left me in peace for several hours. In the afternoon I heard the door
open and thought, "Here we go again." But instead of putting the
hood on me they took me out with my face uncovered, and took me
to two gentlemen whom they said were the judge and the judge's
clerk, and they insisted on asking me whether I wanted to report
anything on the treatment I had received. I didn't trust them and
for a while I wouldn't open my mouth. Finally they convinced me
they really were a judge and clerk and I talked about the torture to
which I had been subjected. They said it wouldn't happen again
and they would give me something to eat and I could get some
sleep and so on. I went back to jail and after a while I fell asleep. I

* Colloquial Spanish for 'I've got guts – you won't get me down'.

was woken up by the order to stand up and turn my back to the door, and then it all started again.'

VI

Enrique Osano was arrested on 8 October 1969 at Toledo Chico, during the withdrawal from Pando.

'What did you do before you joined the organisation?'

'I worked at La Platense [a large commercial establishment].

'At La Platense?'

'What's wrong with that? Aren't La Platense employees allowed to be revolutionaries if they want to, or something?'

'No, no. I didn't mean that. Tell me how you came to be caught.'

'Well – we were behind some bushes at Toledo Chico. By then we didn't have any guns or anything, and we were surrounded by the police. There were several of us. There was a girl there too. I'll never forget her – she was wearing high heels.'

'Did you all know each other?'

'No, none of us in that bunch knew the others.'

'Then how did you know you were all in the same thing?'

'Well – we just knew. We'd seen each other during the Pando operation. We recognised each other because of the white band round our arm.'

'A white band round your arm?'

'Yes – round our left arm. We could hear the police coming – we could see them too – they were still some way away and they were making a circle round us.'

'Did they have dogs with them?'

'No – machine-guns. Just then a helicopter arrived and started to direct operations. I think it was then – at that moment – that we all felt that we might all be wiped out, the lot of us.'

'Why?'

'Because of the way they were doing things. So ruthless somehow. They'd cleared the area; most of the houses were empty. Somebody was giving instructions from the helicopter, through a loudspeaker. It was just like a military operation in wartime. And they raked the fields with gunfire, regardless. Not aiming at anything particular, just firing. That's how I copped it in the leg.'

'Was it you that David Melian found on the floor in a pool of blood when they got out of the lift at Police Headquarters?'

'That's right – that was me. Well, after they got me in the leg I decided to scarper. It wasn't easy, the wound was in my knee. I tried to go in the opposite direction to where the firing was coming from. But I was unlucky – it just wasn't my day. I ran into a much bigger bunch of them than the other one.'

'What had the first lot been – the ones you were trying to get away from?'

'Metropolitan Guard.'

'And this new lot?'

'There were several – some were Highway Patrol, Radio Patrol, Metropolitan Guard – all sorts. When I saw I was surrounded I decided to give myself up. I put my hands up behind my head and walked out into the open and shouted that I was surrendering, that I was wounded and that I was unarmed. Down in a dip a car was standing and sitting back in it was a policeman from Radio Patrol. I started to walk towards him with my hands holding the back of my head. He didn't even move, just lifted his revolver and fired at me as if he'd been doing target practice.'

'Did he hit you?'

'No.'

'How far away was he?'

'Oh – seventy or eighty metres.'

'Did he really mean to hit you, do you think?'

'Oh yes. The bullets whistled past on both sides of my head. One went through the crook of my arm, between my elbow and my ear.'

'When you realised he was firing to kill, why didn't you throw yourself on the ground?'

'Because I'd heard a couple of policemen saying that they'd finish off anybody who fell.'

'When did you hear that?'

'When we were in the bushes. Two of them were going around firing into the bushes and undergrowth to catch anybody who might be lurking and they were talking together. One said, "If you bring any of these sons of bitches down, just polish them off." And the other one said OK, he would. The words stuck in my mind and later on I thought to myself, "Whatever happens I must keep on my feet".'

'Did you manage to?'

'Not all the time. To go back to when I was giving myself up; I moved on again after a minute, very carefully. The chap who'd shot at me started to reload, but somebody went up to him and stopped him.'

'Did he give him an order?'

'No – he struggled with him for a while, grabbed him by the arm. Then some others joined them and I realised they were all arguing. I couldn't hear what they were saying. Anyway, finally they took him away.'

'Who was it who stopped him?'

'In the first place one of the Highway Patrol. Well – just after this a lot of the Metropolitan Guard carrying machine-guns loomed up all over the place.'

'And that was when you were taken?'

'Yes – kicking and pushing me they took me to a ditch and knocked me into it with a blow on the head with a rifle butt – and then they started on me.'

'They started to beat you?'

'Yes – they kicked me and punched me – they went on and on.'

'How many of them were there?'

'How should I know? It was hellish. More of them kept arriving in cars and other vehicles. Army men, Radio Patrol, Metro.'

'Highway Patrol too?'

'No – they didn't join in.'

'They didn't?'

'No – and they not only didn't join in, they looked on as if they were surprised and disapproving.'

'Why do you think there should be such a difference between the ordinary police and the Highway Patrol?'

'I suppose it could be because the Highway Patrol doesn't really have much to do with crime. They've a completely different job to do in society so I suppose they've got a different outlook.'

'Do you think that the rest of the police, because they are constantly in touch with crime, end up by resembling the criminals they have to deal with?'

'I don't know – could be – I know there's often not much difference. But the Metros – the Metropolitan Guard – they're not like anybody. They're a peculiar phenomenon – way-out, very extreme.'

'Do you mean they stand out because they're irrational and violent?'

'They're certainly that, although maybe their irrationality worries me more than their violence. I'd say they're more like robots than humans.'

'What happened after they'd taken away the man with the revolver?'

'More and more vehicles kept arriving – more and more men came and had a bash at me. Then I saw one of them – just an ordinary policeman, I think he was from up-country – aiming at me with a Mauser.'

'How did you know he was from up-country?'

'By the look of his jacket and his funny accent. Anyway he pressed the gun on my forehead and crying – he was crying like anything, the tears streaming down his face – he told me I was Zabalza* and he had to kill me.'

'I don't understand – what did he say?'

'He said, "You're Zabalza – you son of a bitch – and I've got to kill you." He held the gun just near my face and kept on saying it over and over, and all the time he kicked me.'

'But why Zabalza? I don't understand.'

'Well – he thought I was Zabalza of course. I don't know why they'd want to kill him.'

'And didn't anything happen or anybody say anything to make it clear why they should?'

'No.'

'Did it happen again?'

'Yes, right away. Several other men who were standing around and heard him accuse me of being Zabalza started to jump up and down and shout: "This is Zabalza – Zabalza." As if they'd discovered something wonderful.'

'Then what happened?'

'They pushed away the man who was aiming at me.'

'To stop him firing at you?'

'No – so that they could get at me to hit me. Do I have to go into details?'

* Ricardo Zabalza – son of a Government Counsellor of the same name, on the 'White' side of the Government. Ricardo Zabalza Junior was in fact killed that same day at Toledo Chico.

'I think you ought to – but I leave it to you. Why does it upset you?'

'It makes me feel ill to think about it. I'd rather not.'

'Do you look back on it all as something unreal – like a nightmare?'

'No – quite the reverse – it's too bloody real. I wish I could forget it. I try not to believe or admit that all those things happened to me – that they are part of my life. I wish to God – and I know this isn't very revolutionary of me – that I could wipe it all out.'

'Have you never wondered why?'

'No.'

'So it's just that you don't want to go over all the suffering.'

'No – what's happened has happened. I had to pay my apprenticeship fee as a revolutionary. No – it's not that.'

'I have a theory.'

'Let's hear it.'

'I wonder whether this episode made you doubt very basic things. Like whether life is worth living – whether mankind has any future.'

'Could be – but I know damn well that life's worth living – and that mankind has a future in spite of all this.'

'What happened afterwards?'

'For a while I was the centre of attention. Each new arrival had a go at me.'

'Were you down by this time?'

'I was sitting hunched up with my knees up to my chest trying to protect my face and head behind them. I couldn't really do much though. Two soldiers held me with their boots on either side and a third put his foot on my chest, steadied my head with a stick like somebody getting his eye in for a golf-shot, and then he swung at me and split my head open.'

'Did you faint?'

'I didn't go right off – I was stunned though. Just then I heard orders being given – people were shouting and running. Word was given that the area should be cordoned off because some more of our people were in a hut near by. Those who'd been having their fun with me drifted off but first they shoved me over in the ditch so that I was lying down. Then they put two prison vans along the verge so that I couldn't see the road and nobody on the road could see me. After a few minutes I heard one of the radios in the cars announcing that Zabalza had been killed.

'Right away a young fellow got down from one of the two prison vans and came over to me. He seemed just a kid – his skin was like a baby's, no beard or anything. He had a long ·38 in his hand, and two machine-gun loaders in the other hand. He stopped about half a metre away from me and stood looking at me. "You aren't Zabalza but we're going to kill you just the same," he said, pointing the ·38 at my head and drawing back the safety catch.'

'Was he just like the others – all worked up – hysterical and furiously angry?'

'No – not a bit. He didn't look like a murderer, nor did he look as if he knew what he was doing. I felt he was just functioning like a cog in a gearwheel. He knew he had to do something but had no idea why he had to do it.'

'How did you get that impression?'

'From the way he looked – almost apologetic – as if he had to justify himself. And from his words too.'

'What did he say?'

'"I've got to kill you – I've got to." And then, as if to try and find a way out for himself, "Why did you have to get mixed up in this?"'

'Do you think he wanted you to say something that would justify his killing you?'

'Yes.'

'He wanted a reply that would work him up to the pitch?'

'Yes – he wanted me to say something that would annoy him, infuriate him. So – very gently – I said, "Maybe you're the one that's making a mistake." He said he had a mother, a wife and kids.'

'What did he mean by that?'

'I think he was trying to tell me that he was just doing his job. What he was paid to do.'

'What did you say?'

'I said I too had a wife, a baby on the way, and a mother. I hadn't been found in a cabbage patch.'

'In a cabbage patch? How could you joke at such a time?'

'It wasn't meant as a joke, I can tell you. I was trying desperately to think of the right things to say – to relieve him of his obligation to kill me. I wanted him to pause. I don't know what I wanted – one thinks of so much so quickly – I had to find exactly the right thing to say, nothing else would do.'

'You wanted to shake his convictions – make him hesitate?'

'Yes – confuse him – make him hesitate. He kept putting the safety catch on and off. He looked at me very fixedly but I felt he was looking right through me at something else. He was confused. Then somebody came running up and asked him what he was waiting for – why didn't he get on with it and kill me.'

'You think he'd been ordered to kill you?'

'I haven't the smallest doubt that at that moment his job was to kill me.'

'What did he say to the other man?'

'He seemed gradually to come back to reality. He looked at me again and then turned round and started to say something to the man who'd come running up. I couldn't hear what he said.'

'Couldn't you hear anything at all?'

'No – they talked very low – whispering. You're always trying to find out about fear, about what one feels when one is afraid: well, I can tell you, while those two unknown men talked, I was dreadfully afraid. I knew that whether I lived or died depended on what they said . . . they were deciding my fate . . .'

'Why don't you go on?'

'That's the bit I remember most clearly, but I can't really describe what I felt – I was going to die there – with my hands tied – unable to defend myself. In a millionth of a second all sorts of things went through my head. They always say that a drowning man sees his whole life in one blinding flash. I know just how it is. I thought about those I love. My pregnant wife, my mother . . .'

'Did you think of things you'd done in your life?'

'Yes – I remembered when I'd had a collision on my motor-bike and I flew about 20 metres through the air. I remembered every detail. I remembered being five years old and not quite as tall as the dining-room table and asking my mother when I'd be able to see on top of the table. And all these things – flashbacks I suppose they were – all mixed up with what we had just been doing in Pando. As if everything had all been happening at the same time.'

'What did they decide?'

'He was ordered to go ahead – he had to kill me.'

'You actually heard the order given?'

'Yes – the other fellow said, "Let him have it – go on – don't be scared."

'The young one pointed his gun at me again. He crouched down on his haunches so that we were level. He looked at me – he didn't want to kill me, I could see it in his eyes. His hands trembled – he fingered the safety catch. As it happened, we were both lucky. A Press photographer arrived just then and that saved my life and the young man from becoming a murderer.'

'How was that?'

'Well – by the very fact that somebody else was there. The man who had come to tell the young fellow to get on with it now grabbed him by the shoulder and said, "Leave him be – we can't do it now. We've got the Press here." My would-be murderer closed his eyes and lowered his gun. I started to laugh – I couldn't help it – and that's the way I came out in the photographer's picture. It was printed in the *BP*.* There I was, with two policemen holding me up by the armpits, and me laughing. Well, you see, I'd just been reborn. All the same – it's sort of strange.'

'What is?' – OF COURSE IT WAS, STUPID!

'I was so happy to have been saved. So glad to be alive.'

'So I should think.'

'Yes, it was natural, I suppose. But what I find so odd is that from then on I've stopped worrying about life – about living. I haven't been afraid again. I think maybe you can only once in your life be really afraid of dying.'

'What happened afterwards?'

'Well – I was dragged out of the ditch, and practically carried along by the police – two of them – then I saw Otero's red car coming along the road. He had his whole contingent in tow.'

'Investigaciones?'

'Yes – him and his usual string of clerks and junior police officers. He slewed his car across the road and stopped, then he got out. There were two of our people in his car – they'd just been arrested.'

'What did Otero do?'

'Otero went about his business while the two policemen who had dragged me along by the armpits sat me down in the road, with my back propped against the left wheel of the red car.'

'Why was that?'

* A journal of the parliamentary opposition.

'So they'd be able to hit me more comfortably, I suppose – I don't know. I only know that they started to punch me and kick me again.'

'What about Otero?'

'Oh, he dissociated himself from the whole thing – as if it was nothing to do with him. They broke two of my ribs and all my teeth were knocked loose. I couldn't eat for a month.'

'Was a medical report attached to the official report on you?'

'I don't think so. But they've got X-ray photographic records at the Military Hospital.'

'What happened then?'

'They kicked me along, rolling me over and over, until I was off the road. When I could lift my head I could see Zina Fernandez, the Chief of Police, coming along – he had a Luger in his right hand, his jaw was clenched, his eyes very wide open. He came up to me and asked me what was going on and why was I screaming. I looked at him and shut up.'

'Why did you shut up?'

'Well – his question was so bloody stupid. He could see what was going on.'

'What did he do then?'

'He shrugged his shoulders and walked away. He'd hardly turned his back when the two policemen started on me again.'

'They kept on hitting you?'

'Yes, until they got tired. When they got tired they dragged me across the road to the embankment on the other side. A private green van was parked there, a Chevrolet 57. They'd diverted it off the road because the road was blocked by Otero's car. At that point they took the handcuffs off and put them back on my right hand leaving my left hand free.'

'Why free one of your hands?'

'I didn't know – then – but I did soon after. An officer came up to me, he had a Star Machine-gun in his hands and he told me to push off. "Go on," he said, "you're free." "What about you?" I said. "Me?" he said. "Yes, you," I said. "You go – I don't want to go anywhere." But he kept on.'

'What did he say?'

'He kept insisting that I was free and that I should go.'

'He wanted you to appear to be trying to escape so that he would be justified in shooting you – was that it?'

'Yes – that was it all right. But it didn't work. I stayed right where I was, I didn't move as much as a finger. If he wanted to kill me he'd have to kill me right there – I wasn't going to give him an alibi. I then felt an awful blow on my head and I fell forward. I learned afterwards that I'd been hit with a ·38.'

'How did you know that?'

'By the shape of the hole in my scalp. The hole made by the chain the police hook onto the butt of the revolver.'

'What happened afterwards?'

'One of them stood on me and handcuffed my hands behind my back. I had my head in the rut that the van had made in the earth of the embankment.'

'Where was the van driver?'

'In the cab. He'd been ordered not to get out. I was facing the wheel when I heard the officer order the man to back the van.'

'How far were you from the wheel?'

'Half a metre – I was looking at it. I really couldn't look at anything else but although my eyes were glued to the tyre I couldn't say whether it moved at all or not. I just know. I heard the officer repeat the order to the man to back his van. Then I saw that the driver was opening the cab door and then I saw him running away full pelt. I never saw his face nor anything else about him except his clothes. He was wearing a dark-red checked shirt and blue trousers. Several policemen started to run after him. If they'd caught him they'd have taken him apart. They didn't bother to find out whether a man belonged to our lot or not, they'd just lay into him.'

'And weren't you scared during this particular episode?'

'No – I really don't think I'll ever be scared again. By then I'd accepted the fact of death – of my death – as part of the pro-gramme.'

'A revolutionary's programme?'

'That's right. You sometimes need to go through an experience like I went through to really bring it home to you.'

'What happened then? The plan to squash you flat with the van having misfired, what did they do next?'

'They started to kick me again. I remember that I rolled over and managed to sit up, and I made myself as small as I could so there'd be less of me exposed for kicking but as I now had my hands fastened behind my back I couldn't really protect myself much. A COPSA bus came along the road just then. All the passengers leaned out of the windows and started to shout at the police, "Murderers, murderers." I could hear them quite clearly. Somebody came running to move Otero's car so that the bus could go by. Whilst this was being done the people in the bus kept shouting. I don't know whether it was because of the bus incident but it had hardly gone on its way when two of Otero's men came along and said they would take charge of me.'

'Did they seem less brutal than the others?'

'I thought so at first but I soon found out differently.'

'Do you mean they just wanted to have a turn at beating you up?'

'More or less. They took me to one of the police cars and made me get in and the first thing was that they gave me a thundering great punch in the belly. Then as the car went on its way to Police Headquarters the man sitting next to me began to examine my head and suddenly he tapped my ear and said, "Look – here's a bit with no blood on it – can't have that," and gave me such a swipe I think I shall be deaf for the rest of my days.'

'What happened when you arrived at Headquarters?'

'Oh – the usual pack drill. As soon as they realised that I could hardly walk because I had a bullet in my knee they forced me to kneel. They kept banging my face against the wall and saying, "You've got to be a good little boy and do as you're told." Just as they had forced me down on my knees Otegui arrived.'

'Who is Otegui?'

'He's a very important man at headquarters. They call him "el pocho". He came up to me and said in a very sweet voice, "I say, blondie – what are you doing kneeling there." He made me get up and then sit on the floor, and took the handcuffs off me. I just lay there in a great pool of blood, a laughing-stock for all the police who arrived.'

'Why?'

'Oh – they thought they'd laugh at me, I suppose. They called out to each other to come and look and they all laughed. "You're going to die like a rat," they said. "You're bleeding to death – just look at the pool of blood getting bigger and bigger."'

'Didn't you come into contact with policewomen at all?'

'You think they'd act differently?'

'Yes – I do.'

'Well, I can tell you that whilst I was lying there in the pool of blood about a dozen or so women police constables came in from the street.'

'What did they look like?'

'They're quite incredible. Attractive; smartly dressed. They laughed loudest. Particularly when Otegui came up and tore off my trouser leg from the knee down so that they could have a better look at the wound. At that point they all applauded. They shouted to each other to come and look at me taking my last gasp. "Come and see," they called, "he can't have any blood left." Then suddenly, from somewhere a doctor and a nurse appeared and looked at my wounds and said I'd have to be taken away. Otero said they'd do it later, they didn't have anybody available to take me right then.'

'Was that a lie?'

'I'll say! The place was crawling with policemen.'

'When did they finally take you away?'

'Some time after seven.'

'They took you to the Military Hospital?'

'That's right. They sent me off with two very young policemen – cadets – two greenhorns who lectured me, talking of law and order and so on. I was past caring or arguing, I could scarcely open my mouth. I let them talk.'

'And what were you thinking?'

'I was sorry for them.'

'Why? Because they were so young?'

'Yes, I think that sort of wrong thinking can have more effect on very young people.'

'What happened when you got to the hospital?'

'They took me along to a room to give me some preliminary first aid and tidy me up a bit. The nurse told the two young men from Investigaciones to leave me alone.'

'And what did they do?'

'They stuck fast. They'd been ordered not to leave me alone for a minute and they were carrying out their orders. The nurse finally ignored them and started to wash the wounds on my head carefully. Whilst she was washing me she asked why there was so much mud and grass mixed with the blood. At this stage a doctor arrived. He told the nurse sharply to lay me face down on the bed and to put an operating gown over me. Then he made the nurse go away and told the two young policemen to come up. He would show them how to suture a wound . . .'

'Why do you stop? What did the young men do?'

'Nothing – they drew near to watch.'

'And the doctor?'

'He started to stick the needle in as if he were sewing me up.'

'How do you mean? As if he were sewing you up?'

'Well – there wasn't any thread or whatever they use to sew one up.'

'That can't be true. No – you must have been half senseless with all the knocking about you'd had – you couldn't surely even have known who you were by then. You were unconscious, surely.'

'No.'

'No what?'

'I never lost consciousness.'

'Then that couldn't have been a doctor. It must have been another policeman.'

'The nurse always addressed him as Doctor.'

'Would you know him again if you saw him?'

'I never saw his face – but I know who it was.'

'Tell me.'

'No – not yet.'

'That's a pity. But you know who it is, that's something. What did the two young men do meanwhile?'

'The two police cadets? Oh, they came up and killed themselves laughing.'

'What did you do?'

'Me? Nothing – I shut up. I could feel the needle going through and I could feel my temple throbbing and a thread of hot blood trickling over my face.'

'What were you thinking?'

'You won't believe me, I know, but I was thinking of all those things that lead a man to become a revolutionary.'

'And did that help you?'

'Yes, it helped.'

Rodabel Cabrera was arrested on 8 March 1970, accused of harbouring in his house two of the thirteen girls who had escaped from the women's prison on 6 March of the same year.

Questioned on the details of the torture to which he was subjected, Cabrera replied quietly, unemotionally, as if he were talking about something which had happened to somebody else whom he barely knew.

'Why do you think they tortured you so viciously?'

'They thought I was an important member of the movement.'

'How did you know this?'

'When I arrived at Police Headquarters I was taken to Moran Chaquero's* office and he said: "If you are honest you must acknowledge how deeply you are involved in all this."'

'And what did you say?'

'I said that the full extent of my involvement was that I belonged to the organisation and had given shelter in my house to two fellow members who had escaped from prison. He then said it couldn't be just that, and that I was important.'

'What happened then?'

'For a while he kept on and on insisting that I was important and I would deny it. I'm not important.' He spoke in a low voice as if talking to himself.

'He didn't believe you?'

'No. He called Deputy Beson and handed me over to him. Whilst I was being led away to the cell he said, "As you won't talk you're going to dream."'

'What did he mean by that?'

'I didn't know at first. They took me into the cell and the jailer put a bandage round my eyes and a hood over my head right down to my shoulders. The bandage was wet. The hood was damp and dirty. Everything smelt damp and dirty.'

'Was this when you realised what he'd meant by "going to dream".'

'I realised they were going to torture me. They took me out of

---

* Moran Chaquero was executed by the Tupamaros on 13 April 1970.

174

the cell and ran me around for a long time, up and down passages and corridors turning me right round, making me stoop as if I was going through a very low doorway.'

'How long did all this last?'

'I don't know – four or five minutes. I don't remember. Then in one of the corridors they took all my clothes off and four men got hold of me and wrapped wet rags around my wrists and ankles.'

'Was that to increase the effect of the electric current?'

'No – it was to prevent the straps which held me down leaving any marks.'

'Did they peg you down on an iron grid?'

'No, I was fastened down on a mattress on the floor. A wet mattress. My arms were crossed over my body and my legs pegged out apart.'

'And then they began to question you again?'

'Yes. To question and to give me electric shocks.'

'What did they ask you?'

'"Where are the others?" they'd ask. "Where are the others, you son of a bitch?" And they'd apply the electric current to my privates.'

'What else did they say?'

'They told me I'd never make love again. They'd leave me useless.'

'In those very words?'

'No. They put it more crudely.'

'Did you believe they would maim you for life?'

'Yes. I was sure of it. Have you ever imagined what it feels like to have an electric shock applied to your . . . body?'

'I suppose it must be like catching hold of a live wire with your fingers.'

'That's what I used to think, but I can tell you it's nothing like the real thing. One could bear that, but this is quite different. A million times worse. If they give you a shock to the sexual organs you feel as if they're dragging your kidneys and bladder out with a pair of tongs. The effect of electricity is increased in the parts of the body which hold liquids.'

'Did they only apply electric shock to your genitals?'

'At first they ran the electrode over my whole body. When it goes close to the heart you can't speak or breathe, you're paralysed.

They keep wet rags over you all the time to increase the effect. When the rags dry off they wet them again.'

'What other questions did they put to you apart from wanting to know the whereabouts of the escaped girls?'

'They asked me for names of people at Police Headquarters who were passing information to the organisation about impending raids on people's houses.'

'I suppose if you hadn't been in such a ghastly situation you would have found their questions odd, perhaps even amusing. Is there somebody inside the police passing out information, and does this worry them?'

'Yes, they're worried too because police officials supply material for falsifying documents.'

'Oh, so that material comes from Police Headquarters, does it?'

'It would seem so, at least that's what they were saying.'

'What else did they say?'

'They said, "Nobody saw us arresting you and bringing you here."'

'Meaning "We can kill you and nobody will know"?'

'That's right. They said "You can die right here and nobody will ask us anything about it."'

'Did you believe them?'

'Well – it wasn't exactly true that they wouldn't have to account to anybody for their actions, but they weren't to know that.'

'And was their feeling of security – though false – dangerous for you?'

'I thought so at the time.'

'You wouldn't have been the first to die under their ministrations. What else did they say?'

'You want to know what other questions they asked me?'

'No, I want to know what else they said about the whole torture business.'

'They said they wouldn't mind leaving me dead.'

'Just like that, eh?'

'Just like that.'

'What does the electrode – the instrument of torture – look like?'

'It must be a flexible bit of wire with a knob on the end because when I arched under the effect of the shock I can't remember anything rigid sticking into me anywhere.'

'Did you never actually see it?'

'No.'

'Or the man who was doing this to you?'

'No – I never saw him either.'

'Would you have liked to?'

'What – see his face, you mean?'

'Yes.'

'I think I would have.'

'There are rumours about who it is who does this.'

'There must be more than one.'

'Agreed – but the rumours are about one definite person.'

'Yes – I know.'

'Did you scream much?'

'Other members who heard me say that some of the ordinary prisoners had tears streaming down.'

'So you did scream.'

'I yelled like a stuck pig. It's a pain like nothing else. Quite unbelievable. More painful than just pain.'

'How long did the session last?'

'According to those who heard my screams it went on for more than an hour. But I couldn't tell you. I passed out more than once. I lost all sense of time. Once, when I was coming round I heard somebody shouting down the corridor to the torturer: "Hi there! The Chief's been on to the Minister. He says you can pull all the stops out on this one, it won't matter if you do him in. He hasn't got any family to complain."'

'They said a lot about nobody knowing you were there? That nobody would complain?'

'Yes, this threat came turn and turn about with the questions on where the girls were and who it was who gave information from police headquarters. Questions, threats and electric prods until finally they gave up and dragged me away.'

'Were you able to leave under your own steam, so to speak?'

'No – two of them dragged me away. I couldn't walk. And I'd screamed so much I'd practically lost my voice. It was all thick as if I was drunk.'

'Where did they take you?'

'They handcuffed me again and put me back in the cell. After half an hour they took me back to the office to Beson and Villar, the two deputies.'

'Did the interrogation continue?'

'Yes, they kept repeating the same questions as when they'd been giving me the electric shocks. And when my answers didn't satisfy them they punched me in the stomach. They had a couple of junior men in the room who would take it in turn to punch me one after another.'

'How long did this go on?'

'The first time not so long – but they took me back there five or six times at least.'

'And it was always the same?'

'Yes – always – a question and punch, punch and then another question.'

'Did they take off your handcuffs this time?'

'No – they only took them off when they were giving me the electric shocks.'

'So you had them on from five on Saturday morning . . .'

'. . . right through until three on Monday afternoon when I went up before the judge.'

'What happened when you went to the lavatory?'

'They didn't take me to the lavatory.'

'How did you appear before the judge?'

'Need I say? I had to apologise. I was a filthy wreck and trembling from head to foot. I could hardly walk.'

'Why were you trembling?'

'I suppose because of the electric shocks – and the punchings and having no rest. My arms were so swollen through the handcuffs being tight that I couldn't lift them up.'

'What did the judge do?'

'He had a doctor called. I wasn't interrogated until he'd seen me.'

'Was there any difference between your first statement at Police Headquarters and the statement you made to the judge?'

'None at all. I belong to the NLM, and I said so. I sheltered two girl members and I told them that too. There wasn't anything more to say, so I didn't say it.'

Escapes

It was one of those cold, sunny winter days so typical of Montevideo. The Director of Penal Institutes was enjoying a peaceful breakfast. He had had a cup of bitter maté, made a routine telephone call to his office to check that all was well 'Everything OK?' he'd asked. 'Yes – all OK here, came the reply. At peace with the world he put down the receiver and sat himself down in front of a steaming cup of coffee, reaching slowly for the butter to spread on his toast. Then the telephone rang and his peaceful world disintegrated around his ears, at the sound of an anonymous voice saying, 'Colonel Cirilo? Sendic* escaped this morning in a dust cart.' 'In a dust cart? Who's that speaking?' Cirilo's peace of mind and appetite disappeared in one fell swoop. A pitiless click was all the reply instrument would yield. Abandoning his coffee and his enraptured contemplation of a beautiful morning, he flew to his office, a building surrounded by seven-foot high walls. Trying to conceal his anxiety he went through to the prison precinct. 'Sendic?' the jailer answered in astonishment. 'In his cell of course.' Further questions: 'No, sir, no, there could be no contact between the prisoners and the dust carts. It would be very difficult – quite impossible, sir.' 'I want to see him,' snapped Cirilo. He was led to the cell. There he saw the familiar face, the greying hair, the black moustache, the blue eyes, the calm gestures. Standing in the doorway he listened to the man's quiet voice.

He went home mumbling happily to himself.

It was just a little over a year since the thirteen women had escaped from the Cabildo Prison. Thirteen girls really, most of them were between 20 and 23. Their escape had caused an uproar and led to the resignation of a minister who was made the central figure of the scandal. He remembered it all as if it had been yesterday. The shrill, discordant voice of the woman who had witnessed the escape from her place in the front pew in the chapel. She had been quite overcome by the experience. 'There I was, right up front. I had just knelt down. The priest had just taken Communion himself and he was kneeling too – poor Father – he had his head bowed, he was in communion with our Dear Lord . . . and then suddenly, from behind the altar they burst out, and as if that wasn't enough . . .' at that her voice rose to a shrill squeak '. . . as

* Raul Sendic, a reputed founder of the Tupamaros.

181

if that wasn't enough one of *them* appeared at the door at the back, the one that opens onto the street, and he told us to keep quiet – he threatened us.' 'How did he threaten you? What did he say?' She was being filmed during the interview. 'He said what they all say when these things happen – he said "keep quiet and nothing'll happen to you".' 'Can you remember anything special about him?' she was asked. 'He looked just like everybody else – they all look alike.' The interviewer had turned and smiled at the TV cameras at this point. 'Wasn't there anything at all different about him?' he asked. 'Yes,' she beamed helpfully. 'He was holding a gun in his right hand.'

And that was how it had been. The girls had left the prison through the main door of the chapel, and within a few days a shame-faced Minister, held to account by Parliament, was leaving his Ministry by the back door.

Then just a few days ago Almiratti had escaped, from the court itself. And as nobody could explain away this escape except in terms of a plot, all those present were accused of complicity, court officials, the judge, guards, the lawyer, everybody. The city buzzed. First one and then another preposterous rumour went the rounds. 'The guards had been in league with the prisoner and fired into the air.' 'The lawyer was a Tupamaro himself and released him.' 'The court officials had cleared a way for him to the door of the court.' 'The judge had accepted a bribe of 50 – 60 – 70 million pesos to look the other way.' And so on.

Colonel Cirilo himself didn't believe a word of it. He thought the prisoner had simply acted swiftly, relying on the paralysing effect of surprise. The guards had fired the minute they recovered their presence of mind but by then Juan Almiratti had had a fair start and was too far away, and what with the confusion and mortification of seeing their prisoner getting away not one of the bullets had found its mark.

These were the Colonel's thoughts as he crossed the yard back to his own quarters. He called to one of the clerks to bring him coffee and something to eat from the kitchen. Then he sat down to have his breakfast. 'Sendic escaping in a dust cart! That would have been the last straw,' he thought. 'Almiratti was more than enough!'

He wasn't to know that Almiratti was only the beginning. The forerunner of a series of escapes. Within ten days one hundred and fifty were to escape.

Raul Bidegain Greissing

For two years the newspapers had been full of his doings. No important exploit took place without – according to the Press – Bidegain having a hand in it. 'Bidegain, wielding a sub-machine-gun, overcame the porter.' 'Bidegain ordered them all to turn and face the wall.' 'Bidegain lit the fuse.' 'Bidegain covered the retreat with a pistol in his hand.' Bidegain, always Bidegain. For eighteen months any thin, fair-haired man taking part in guerrilla activities was bound to be reported as Bidegain. Then came a day when he really was in the news – he had been captured. The report stated: 'Today Sendic, La Rey, Candan Crajales and Bidegain Greissing were captured.'

Bidegain, 23 years old, whose grandparents had been Basque-French, thin, fair-haired, blue-eyed, laughed an ironic, boyish laugh when questioned about his supposed exploits. Humped in a chair, jerking his head nervously, shifting one way and another, he told the court casually that he had indeed been the moving spirit in all these exploits. He said the gun was for the young. The old weren't fit to be revolutionaries.

'Who are the old?' he was asked.

'Anybody over 40 is old,' said he, enjoying the look of annoyance on the face of the 43-year-old lawyer.

On 8 August 1970 he had been captured. On 17 July 1971 he left the prison by his own means, without help of lawyers or machine-guns. He walked out quite openly through the main gates. Back in his cell he left as hostage his 18-year-old brother. A hundred eyes watched him escape and never saw him, warders, common prisoners, political prisoners, families visiting their relatives in jail. Questioned closely they all said the same. They'd seen nothing, hadn't noticed the switch. Nobody knew anything. The long table in the visitors' hall had been packed. Ranged on one side were the prisoners, opposite them their wives, mothers, children. Right at the end Raul Bidegain sat on one side, thin, tall, with short fair hair, 23 years old. Opposite him sat his brother, Gabriel Bidegain, thin, tall, with short fair hair, 18 years old.

When visiting time finished the two brothers hugged and said

good-bye. One stayed, the other left. The one who left picked up
the usual exit permit. Before leaving the prison he was subjected
to the usual careful search. Alas, however, the Forces of Law and
Order, as so often before, were wrong. They let out the one who
should have been inside.

Raul stepped out on the pavement in Calle Ellauri, breathed
deeply, looked up at the overcast sky, sniffed the cold air blowing in
from the coast and plunged into the hospitable, protective friendly
city of Montevideo, founded some two hundred years before by
Don Bruno Mauricio de Zabala, and lost himself among its
1,300,000-odd inhabitants.

Thirty-eight women

It was about nine o'clock in the evening. The guards, wrapped
to the ears in their ponchos in the cold night air, walked around
the well-lit streets surrounding the Women's Prison. Inside its
walls 42 political prisoners were already in bed and all that could
be heard in the dormitory was the sound of their deep breathing. A
wardress carried out a routine check, going around all the beds.
Everybody was sound asleep, even the baby born to one of the
women slept snuggled close to the woman's body.

At eleven o'clock one of the women prisoners called out to the
wardress and asked for an aspirin – she had a headache she said.
When the wardress took it to her she asked, 'What time's your next
round?' 'At five o'clock.' 'Be a dear and wake me,' said the prisoner.
'I want to start work early.'

Around three o'clock in the morning 38 of the women were up
and dressed. Some kept watch whilst others held blankets over the
floor to muffle the sound of the tiles being forced up from underneath. They were all wearing slacks which would make it easy for
them to walk astride the stream of filth flowing down the middle of
the sewers.

One by one the 38 went down through the hole which had been
made in the floor and disappeared in the maze of sewers under the
city leading out to sea.

At five o'clock the wardress came into the dormitory carrying
her torch. She played the light over the beds and saw the shapes in
bed and hair on the pillows. She stopped alongside the bed of the

woman who wanted to be wakened and played the light on her. She didn't move. The shape under the bedclothes didn't stir. The wardress swung the torch round, there were no faces, only shapes and hair.

The morning papers reported that the wardress, suddenly apprehensive, started to pull back the bedclothes. Underneath were pillows, bundles of clothes – an occasional wig. Of the 42 prisoners there were four left. The one with the baby, one who was pregnant and two others whose reasons for staying were not discovered.

By half past five the alarum was in full cry. The area around the prison was filled with hideous noise, sirens wailed, hooters hooted, car engines burst into life and the insides of the sewers were swept by powerful beams of light. Every manhole along the sewerage network was manned by soldiers armed to the teeth, soldiers who for several hours, cold and disgruntled, played at being soldiers. But the sewers had long since been empty and the powerful search-lights only disturbed the occasional innocent rat.

One hundred and six men

Sunday, 5 September, dawned cloudy and dull, with a chill persistent drizzle. The morning papers carried the following weather forecast: sky overcast, low cloud ceiling, isolated showers, temperature rising. They also carried the following official announcement:

Communiqué No 27: Warning to the public: the Ministries of the Interior and Defence, being responsible for the maintenance of Law and Order in the Republic, wish to alert the public in regard to a wave of escalating violence throughout the country aimed at fostering a climate of insecurity and chaos as part of a general plan to overthrow the legally constituted government. The authorities whose duty it is to preserve the security of the State are regretfully forced into the position of having to counter violence with violence.

The day wore on like any other quiet, dull Sunday towards the end of winter. But as the hours went by, swiftly, silently, invisibly, 200 guerrillas, especially trained in the difficult art of achieving a maximum effect with a minimum of violence had acted. Fifteen vehicles were expropriated, quietly, unobtrusively. The bag consisted of ten cars, two buses, two lorries and a motor-scooter.

6.30 pm, Sunday, 5 September

Maria del Carmen Beretta Curi, with a couple of young friends, called on her uncle, the Notary Public, José Curi Zagia. Maria del Carmen, 23 years old, ex-student, was one of the 38 women who had escaped from the women's prison on 30 July. She had been on the run since 1969 and was arrested in February 1971. She had aroused the suspicions of the police when she had been hanging around the house where Lieutenant Dos Santos, murderer of Tupamaro Marcos Larrosa, lived.

The three entered the house and, once inside, told the five occupants that the house was to be used for an operation. They told everybody to keep calm and warned that they were armed, though no guns were seen.

The back of the house was approximately 50 metres from the walls of the Punto Carretas Prison.

7.00 pm

Two young men knocked at the door of Billy Rial's flat. One of them was carrying a stethoscope so Billy thought he must be a doctor. Later, in his statement, he said that the two young men had been friendly but firm. They told him they were Tupamaros and needed the house for a few hours for a special operation. They said they were armed though he didn't see any guns. Hard on the heels of the two young men a girl arrived and the three together asked Billy to go with them to the house next door, the back of which adjoined his flat. They wanted Billy to explain to the two women occupants what it was all about. As the women knew him they wouldn't be frightened. He agreed and followed by the three he knocked at the door. When it was opened he explained to the women that his companions were Tupamaros and were carrying out an operation. He invited them back to his flat to stay until the operation was over. Once in Billy's flat the Tupamaros told the women not to be frightened and to keep quiet. 'Don't go out of the room and nothing'll happen to you,' they said. 'After that,' said Billy, 'they hardly said anything except when they wanted to pacify the women in my flat. There were six all told, my mother and fiancée who had come back from a walk, and two women neighbours who'd called, and of course the two women from next door.' One of the neighbours, when she heard what was going on said, 'Oh, but they can't carry out an operation, the street's alive with prison guards patrolling.' One of the Tupamaros then said, "Don't worry, we'll get them out from under.' 'The woman didn't seem to catch on,' said Billy, 'but I realised that my suspicions that it was a prison escape they were planning was right.'

7.30 pm

More members of the NLM arrived in an estate van at the first house seized, the Curi house. The vehicle was put in the garage and several parcels containing ammunition, documents, revolvers and bundles of money were unloaded. The lot was distributed in polythene bags and laid out neatly on the dining-room table.

8.30 pm

A group of people came running down the Avenida Carlos Maria Ramirez. It was only on the following day that it was realised that they were Tupamaros. They were rowdy and disorderly. They surrounded a bus, threatened the driver with a gun, made the passengers get out and set the bus on fire with petrol bombs. They did the same to four other buses. Others meanwhile gathered heaps of inflammable material and set it on fire. Barricades were thrown up across the ends of roads leading into the Avenida to stop police vehicles getting through. Altogether the disturbances lasted some three hours. Later it was suggested that their purpose had been to concentrate police attention well away from the area where the escape operation was in progress.

9.00 pm

At the local church hall near the prison, not far from where the tunnel was to end, a dance was getting under way. People in the neighbourhood afterwards said that the orchestra, which always played at these dances, played more enthusiastically and noisily that evening and that the racket was worse than usual. Some surmised later that all this extra noise had had the ulterior motive of covering the sounds of underground activity.

Monday, 6 September

3.00 am

Talking later to the Press Billy Rial said that at this time the noises from the tunnellers under the floor was so great that he feared the whole adventure must have a tragic end. At this time too he of the stethoscope began to listen on the floor to find out exactly where the tunnellers were likely to burst through. For the first time during the whole operation the three showed signs of nervousness. Through their walkie-talkies they were in constant touch with friends, no doubt keeping watch in the attics, peeping down at the road below from behind net curtains.

3.20 am

By now, using a mechanised drill and other tools which were later abandoned, the Tupamaros who had taken Billy Rial's flat and the women's place were working on the flooring, lifting it and the underflooring and digging down in the earth beneath. This work took some time and much effort and caused them a good deal of anxiety. The tunnel had arrived at a point two metres below the floor and about half a metre from the front wall of the house.

3.40 am

Final contact was established with the tunnellers. Up through the hole came the first of the escaping Tupamaros. He was wearing a lamp on his forehead, like a miner, and was covered from head to foot with mud. One hundred and ten men followed him, all as muddy as he. It took fifteen minutes for them all to emerge and as they did they shed their filthy top garments, showing clean clothes underneath. At the rear of Billy's flat the Tupamaros had knocked a hole in the wall into an empty house next door. This empty house gave on to Calle Joaquin Nuñez but it wasn't used for the men to leave for fear of attracting attention if such a number of people should be seen leaving an obviously empty house. Instead they all went through another hole knocked between the empty house and the notary's house – held by the Tupamaros – on the farther side. Here the men filed into the dining-room to pick up the bags containing arms, money, ammunition and false documents. There was one for each.

Immediately one of the girls guarding the Curi family told them,

'I'm going to give you a news scoop. Our friends who were in prison are escaping. Within a few minutes we shall all be gone. You must wait half an hour and then notify the police.'

Similar instructions were being given simultaneously by the Tupamaros in Billy Rial's flat.

4.30 am

Billy Rial telephoned Police Headquarters and told them what had happened. They asked him whether he was sure of what he was saying. 'Of course I'm sure,' he said, 'I saw them with my own eyes.'

5.00 am

As half an hour went by and still there was no sign of the police, Billy, with the mouth of the tunnel gaping wide in his sitting-room floor, rang them again. The police told him they had called the prison and nobody there knew anything about an escape. Billy, disheartened, went out to the street and called out to one of the prison guards patrolling along the top of the wall, 'Hey – The Tupamaros have escaped.'

'Go back to bed – you're drunk,' shouted back the guard.

6.00 am

An hour later the police, at last convinced that something had happened, appeared at the houses which had been held by the Tupamaros. A sergeant, gazing disconsolately at the gaping hole, 60 cm by 60 cm, in the floor, and at the drill, spade, pick and pile of muddy garments, exclaimed, 'Four years of work got away through there!'

9.00 am

Although none of the morning papers mentioned the escape the whole of Montevideo knew of it by now. Public imagination was aroused by the exploit and the escapees were heroes. Jokes about them were bandied about, especially one involving a play on the words of an old Sendic slogan, current when Sendic had been a leader in his province: 'If you rely on Sendic and work the good earth you'll go far.' The 'in' joke now was soon: 'Do you know how the Tupamaros escaped?' 'No.' 'They relied on Sendic, worked the good earth and went far.' —HA! very good

As from noon the citizens of Montevideo were blitzed with communiqués:

> Communiqué No 7: Issued by the Ministry of the Interior: A patrol of the Forces of Law and Order stopped a van and detained the two occupants who were said to be carrying subversive literature. Soon afterwards twenty-seven people were detained. There was evidence that some of them were important members of the subversive organisation NLM.

Those detained and the subversive literature were all taken before a judge who could find no reason for proceeding against them. The literature was not as subversive as the police would have wished and the detainees proved to be young people who had attended the church hall dance but had had nothing whatever to do with the escape. Subsequently the Directorate of Penal Institutes thought fit to issue its own Communiqué No 27, as follows:

> The Directorate General of Penal Institutes hereby announces that at dawn to-day 111 detainees held at Punta Carretas Prison escaped through a tunnel. The entrance to the tunnel is in a ground-floor cell of the prison. The outlet is in an apartment building in Calle Solano Garcia. The length of the tunnel is approximately 60 metres. The occupants of the apartment building and of two other buildings adjoining it at the rear but facing on to Calle Joaquin Nuñez were all kept prisoners inside their flats or apartments by armed members of the same organisation to which the escapees belonged. Of the latter 106 were political prisoners and 5 were common criminals.

7 *September*

The Ministries of the Interior and of Defence put out five communiqués. In these they exhorted, begged, threatened and cajoled the public. Messages were addressed to citizens and noncitizens about all kinds of things: about the erosion of individual rights; about the loss of freedom, and the dangers of sedition. The 'gravity of the situation' was dwelt upon and promises made about a firm hand in dealing with chaos and violence. 'The conspiracy is serious and its aims immoral,' they announced solemnly. 'But even in adversity the Government would do its duty.' Moreover, 'any

citizen who took the trouble to analyse the measures adopted –
objectively and in good faith – would be reassured that nothing
had changed and that nothing would change, everything was under
control.'

In fact nothing has changed. The police continue to kill innocent
citizens and students; continue to put into concentration camps
all those who might obstruct their ruthless policies. Newspapers
continue to be suppressed. *La Idea*, the most widely read opposition paper, has been shut down. Finally, the official machine, being
cowardly as well as inelegant and stupid, had to find a scapegoat to
carry the can over the escapes: Colonel Cirilo was deprived of his
rank and court martialled.

8 September

The Tupamaros announced in their Communiqué No 11 that
Geoffrey Jackson had been granted amnesty and would soon be set
free.

COMMUNIQUÉ ISSUED BY THE NATIONAL LIBERATION
MOVEMENT
THE FIGHT TO LIBERATE ALL POLITICAL DETAINEES

A year ago we, the Tupamaros, took up the fight on behalf of
the political detainees. We wanted this to be a painless operation
and so we offered to exchange several important captives,
known to be involved in unsavoury activities or representatives
of despotic régimes, for our friends in prison.

The Government, whilst secretly negotiating with us –
though no agreement was ever reached – publicly adopted a hard
line, neatly summarised in the catch phrase 'We do not barter
with criminals'.

So – a year ago – the battle was on. Blood flowed, the country
lived through grim moments. Why? Why?

To-day, a year later, we can claim with legitimate pride that we
have won that particular fight. Almiratti recovered his freedom,
as did Bidegain. Thirty-eight women members walked to
freedom and now one hundred and eleven of our good and loyal
partisans are back in the ranks of the freedom fighters.

The battle was not won without many sacrifices. Hundreds

nd even thousands of Tupamaros were involved. The Government flung down the gauntlet and we took it up. The old rallying slogan passed down to us from our forbears, *a nation is for everybody or it is for nobody*, was the spirit in which we hit back. We are not a people to be pushed around. That same old spirit is the one on which the National Liberation Movement (Tupamaros) is founded.

When circumstances had reached this stage we decided to free Mr Geoffrey Jackson. His detention by the people no longer had any point now that this particular battle had been fought and won. We let him go freely, by the will of the people, despite the fact that we had already started negotiations for his liberation after the public concern expressed by Chile's President, Salvador Allende, and we place it on record that those negotiations, if followed through, would have proved extremely advantageous to us.

We must make it quite clear once and for all that our attitude is geared to a much wider scale of reasons and circumstances, viz:

1. Though we have won the battle on behalf of these political detainees we have not won the war. Many still languish in prison and barracks and the fight must continue unabated.
2. By our action in releasing Mr Geoffrey Jackson we reaffirm our intention of avoiding useless suffering. It is fitting here to point out that we have lately been the victims of attacks and false accusations. We were, for instance, accused of the death of Eselaskas, and later this accusation was proved false, as were also the accusations that we had been responsible for the deaths of two mounted police of the Republican Guard at the Hospital at Pedro Visca. We have also been falsely accused of intending by our activities to prevent the elections taking place in November.

In the meantime Ramos Filippini, Nieto and Sposito have all been murdered, Castagnetto and Ayala have been kidnapped, and daily acts of aggression, threat and assault are perpetuated on people and property and it is well known that all this is the work of the JUP,* and of the police and members of the Depart-

* Juventud Uruguaya de Pie, 'upstanding Uruguayan Youth', a fascist group.

ments of Information and Intelligence acting under the orders of Macchi, Lucas and Castiglioni, and of the Metropolitan Guard on the instigation of, and financed by, the Government.

The purpose of these activities is to confuse the public and create a climate in which it will be easy to deceive them again.

The responsibility for taking things over the borderline into the realm of cruellest violence should rest squarely where it belongs, with officialdom. They are the ones who would like to prevent formal elections.

3. We must clarify our own position regarding the elections. We do not believe they will resolve the country's problems. Nevertheless they must be held, but on a platform which provides guarantees which are at present lacking. To pretend that proper elections can be held under a system of political detentions, Press censorship, suppression of newspapers, systematic persecution of public militants, a total absence of individual rights, and repression and violence practised on all and sundry with the blessing of authority, is simply to practise a monstrous fraud on the people, which is exactly what is being done.

The fight to re-establish these rights and guarantees is the rallying point for all those groups who come together to form the anti-oligarchic coalition known as the Broad Front [Frente Amplio]. The fight has no beginning and no end. Our support for the Broad Front is representative of our positive approach to the elections. It is not us, therefore, who seek to invalidate the polls. Those who wish to do this are the ones who uphold security measures, who wish only their own voice to be heard, who recognise only one set of reasons. Those who beat, torture, kill, imprison, organise terror squads. Those are the only ones conspiring against the elections.

4. The Oligarchy, through its repressive apparatus and using as its mouthpiece the feeble remnants of the Press so far unsuppressed, organises squads who kidnap the families of men in prison, murder students, torture, carry out dynamite attacks against social militants and the political quarters of the Broad Front.

We would have preferred to ignore these sordid provocations so as to keep the climate cool at this difficult time and save embarrassment, but there are limits. Murder cannot continue to be done with impunity for ever. If they persist they will feel our retaliation and they know it. We shall strike back with the full power of the people against all those responsible – whose names and addresses are in our possession. These include the oligarch who, behind the scenes instigated this whole policy; the shitters of printer's ink who use what is left of a muzzled Press to further the campaign of infamy and lies; the members of DAN and LIS, new names for the new squads made up of the same old police agents trained by Mitrione's* successors.

We tell you clearly, if you go on in the way you have started our retaliation will be implacable. Bear it in mind. We never speak in vain.

We fight to liberate all political detainees

A nation is for everybody or it is for nobody

The bearer of this public message is Mr Geoffrey Jackson, freed today by the National Liberation Movement (Tupamaros).

National Liberation Movement (Tupamaros)
Montevideo, 8 September 1971

8.00 pm

At this time the British Ambassador, Mr Geoffrey Jackson, was released in one of the suburbs of Montevideo. Bearded and wearing the same clothes as when he was taken eight months previously, he knocked on the door of the church at Nuevo Paris. A young man opened the door to him and, unrecognised, he was asked in. When the priest arrived he found Jackson sitting in one of the front pews. He asked him what he wanted. Jackson explained who he was and said he wished to confess and take Communion. He duly confessed and took Communion and then, over a cup of coffee, chatted with the priest about the Capuchin Order, to which the Priest belonged and in which the Ambassador had many friends.

Jackson was calm and composed, emerging from his ordeal just as in the old days one always imagined an Englishman would emerge from a difficult situation. The priest asked him whether he wished to notify the authorities and the Ambassador said no, his

* Dan Mitrione, police commissioner, was executed by the Tupamaros.

194

captors had undertaken to advise his Embassy and the Chargé d'Affaires would no doubt soon arrive.

However, the police arrived first and placed the whole area on a war footing. The officer in charge wanted to interrogate Jackson but the latter, just like others released by the Tupamaros, refused to make a statement. 'Any statements considered necessary will be made in due course through my Chancellery,' he said; and added, 'I am quite well and not suffering from the effects of any drug.'

9.00 pm

The Ambassador drove to the British Hospital in the Daimler from which he had been kidnapped. Five minutes later the Ministers for Foreign Affairs and Public Health arrived, but left a few minutes later without having seen the Ambassador. They declared him, however, to be in good health and spirits.

10.00 pm

The Under-Secretary for Public Health called at the hospital and withdrew soon after, having exchanged a few words with the British Chargé d'Affaires, Mr Hennessy. Interviewed by the Press he said, "'I told Mr Hennessy that I am absolutely certain that the British Ambassador knows very well that this was not the work of Uruguayans.'

This sibylline phrase caused great astonishment to many newspaper readers.

11.45 pm

Mr Jackson left the Hospital surreptitiously by a side door and drove to his residence in Parque Jose Batlle y Ordonez.

10 September

All the morning papers recalled the circumstances of the Ambassador's disappearance and mentioned the swift transit through Montevideo, a few days after the kidnapping of Mr Wright Oliver. At the time the latter had told the Press: 'Great Britain and Uruguay are friendly countries and when friends are in difficulties they help each other. I haven't come here to make recriminations but to try and help find a solution.'

However, the only solution that seemed to occur at that time to the British Envoy and the Uruguayan Executive when they put their heads together was to offer eight million pesos to anybody supplying information which would lead them to the captive Ambassador. His Excellency was indeed fortunate that this stupid offer did not put the police on his track. Geoffrey Jackson knows full well that, had he been traced, his captors would inevitably have executed him.

Epilogue

Seen in the context of the general picture of South American politics, the Tupamaros have a curiously transient quality. This may be because they are a revolutionary movement in a modern and, until recently, democratic society, where people tend to think in terms of elections to solve problems, even though they are realistic enough to realise that things have been going wrong for quite a long time and that some pretty drastic action is required if the population as a whole is going to awake to the desperate plight of the country and the need to change the old, comfortable, traditional type of political party, who think that all must be for the best in the best of all possible worlds.

Most of the really sophisticated South American countries, including Uruguay, have to live on a knife edge. On the one hand they are now sufficiently mature to realise that the foreign capital so eagerly welcomed in the early days has turned into a ravening beast which tends to gobble up the country's wealth; on the other hand this foreign capital has enriched the privileged few in each country, who feel that their way of life will depart with the foreigner if he is pushed out too hurriedly or harshly. These favoured few in every country tended, and still tend, to preserve their way of life by backing ever more ruthless types of government when possible, under the pretence of combating communism, branding every attempt by the masses to improve their miserable lot as incipient communism.

But basic changes in all these countries are slowly taking place. The ordinary people are becoming much more aware and, more important, there are dissidents within the very bosom of entrenched privilege. The sons and daughters of the ruling despots go to universities in their own countries and abroad, and suddenly appear waving banners and leading student uprisings, or merely espousing causes that will inevitably lead to the toppling of the old semi-feudal systems. — *PATTY HEARST, IS THAT YOU?*

Uruguay's close neighbours are particularly interesting in this respect. Chile has for a good many years been progressing towards freer and more independent forms of government. When her last

President, Frei, the Christian Democrat, was elected, there was much wringing of hands and cryings of woe! woe! Now Allende, a Marxist, a genial, cultured man, is in power, and the Greek chorus has become positively deafening. If he can steer himself through his term of office without allowing himself to be pushed off his course either by the extreme Right, who just plain hate his guts, or the extreme Left who want him to nationalise and throw the landlords out and do everything else overnight, by the time the next elections come round the country will have gone that much further towards a democratic, tolerant type of government, and this type of progress is very difficult to reverse.

Argentina, a much closer neighbour, has been to-ing and fro-ing since the days of Perón, but as military ruler succeeds military ruler, the general picture is one of a leaning towards tolerance. There is a determined coming to grips with problems and a great improvement in the conditions of the workers generally and definitely a chilly, if not entirely cold shoulder has been shown to foreign financial interests in the country.

Then there is Brazil, which has a much more repressive régime and where American influence is very strong. The guerrillas in this country also have a much more ruthless plan of action.

This, then, is the background against which on Sunday, 28 November 1971, Uruguay went to the polls. This could have been an opportunity to write 'finis' to the chronicle of the Tupamaros. Unhappily the results have been inconclusive and now, two months after the elections, the wrangling and recounting of votes drags on, as does the repressive system of government, although no president has yet been named.

On this occasion the two traditional blocks or coalitions, i.e. the Reds (comprising various groups with the Nationalists predominating) and the Whites (various similar groups with the Socialists predominating) have been confronted by a third, new party, the Broad Front. Again this party is made up of various groups, mainly Communists, Socialists, left-wing Christian Democrats, Independents and dissidents from the two historic parties. Its leader is General Liber Seregni, a retired army officer, a non-Marxist and, in fact, until recently a member of the Pacheco Government, from which he withdrew because of disagreements with General Pacheco.

The electoral campaign was watched with keen interest by

Uruguay's neighbours, and by the USA. Chile's Allende expressed the opinion that the Broad Front would carry the day. At the same time it was reliably reported that groups of the Brazilian Army, with the connivance of the USA, were poised on the borders with Uruguay ready to invade should the Broad Front win.

The other parties attacked the Broad Front on the grounds that it was a mainly Communist Party, but in fact only some of the coalition are Communists and the Party is supported by the Tupamaros who are known not to be in favour of the Uruguayan Communist Party.

In the event the Broad Front was fairly quickly out of the running, but despite its brief life of a mere few months as a party it had a remarkable success, polling some 22% of the votes. The figures are not precise and probably never will be, but the percentage is sufficiently high to cause the two major parties to pause and take stock whilst there is yet time, if they want to survive.

President Pacheco, precluded by the Constitution from campaigning personally, had a plebiscite inserted in the poll which would enable him to serve a second term, but there was very little support for this and he quickly abandoned the leadership, nominating Juan Maria Bordaberry to be Presidential candidate for his Party.

At first count it seemed that the ruling Reds (Nationalists) had won, but there were immediate claims and counterclaims of discrepancies in counting the votes and a recount was ordered. Two months later the recount has not yet been completed. Recently the Whites complained that there were several unguarded entrances to the Municipal Stadium in Montevideo where the recount is taking place and that moreover some regions had returned more votes than there were people. There was a good deal of bad feeling and the Whites temporarily withdrew from the recount, bringing the whole procedure to a halt as the Constitution requires that both parties to the dispute be present at the recount.

Counting was later resumed and in *La Prensa*, the Argentine paper, it was reported on 18 January that heated quarrels and punch-ups had broken out in the Stadium and an attempt was made on the life of an ex-deputy. There appear to be still some 100,000 votes in dispute, not through discrepancy but because of being cast in a district other than the voter's legal place of residence. Juan Maria Bordaberry was reputed to only have an advantage of 9,500 votes over his adversary, Wilson Ferreira Aldunate, Leader of the Whites.

Apart from occasional mentions in the Argentine papers nothing definite seems yet to be known about when the final results will be announced and it may be some time before the new Government is confirmed in office. Meanwhile the old Government has retained de facto control of the country and the repressive system continues unabated. One of their first moves was to close down the offices of the Broad Front and block their funds. A left-wing newspaper *El Eco* and its publishers Editorial La Alborada, were closed down in December according to a report in *La Prensa* on the 30th.

The Tupamaros, who perhaps hoped to withdraw from the scene in a blaze of notoriety on the spectacular, Colditz-like rescue of their one hundred and eleven members through a tunnel under the road from the prison, and the happy subsequent release of Sir Geoffrey Jackson, have begun to figure in the Argentine Press again. On 30 December, the day the Broad Front was proscribed, a group entered the Municipal Offices on the seventh floor of the Municipality in Montevideo, in broad daylight, and lifted the plans of the sewerage systems of the city.

Later, on 12 January *La Prensa* carried a report that five (originally reported as seven but subsequently amended to five) Tupamaros had been captured by the police when they raided the home of a man who collected arms, in one of the outlying districts of Montevideo. This abortive exploit could mean that the Tupamaros are intent on replenishing their arsenal and perhaps bodes ill for a peaceful period for Uruguay if the new Government does not institute reforms. Both the traditional Parties are known to include land reform and other vital changes in their programmes, but the Broad Front had a much more radical programme for the general redistribution of wealth and one of their main points was that the enormous sums spent on the machinery of repression should be diverted to welfare.

Should the new Government attempt to continue with the old system it is very likely that the world will hear a great deal more of the Tupamaros, and that there may be more kidnappings and that in general the National Liberation Movement may move into a phase of much more ruthless and determined activity.

Anne Edmondson

Postscript

Later Events

In late December the Tupamaros lifted the truce they had called for the elections. It was already clear that the results would not bring the relief desired by many in Uruguay. The Broad Front had been unsuccessful and its members were soon being harassed. Eventually, after many accusations of irregularities in counting the votes, the coalition of the Red Parties was confirmed in office, with Juan Maria Bordaberry as President-elect. In fact this meant no effective change of government or policy, and the renewed activities of the Tupamaros followed the established pattern of holding up banks and commercial enterprises to obtain money and expose malpractices.

On 28 January 1972 *La Prensa* of Buenos Aires reported the release of Ricardo Ferrés, a rich Uruguayan industrialist, who had been held by the Tupamaros for 291 days (neither the police nor Ferrés' family would say whether a ransom had been paid for his freedom). Ferrés said that he had been greatly helped by the physical exercises taught him by Geoffrey Jackson with whom he shared a room in the 'People's Prison', the Tupamaros hide-out. An official communiqué stated that Ferrés had been lodged alone in 'a nauseating cavern, two metres by one, where he could not see daylight'.

On 12 February the Argentine press reported the kidnapping of Homero Farina, editor-in-chief of *Accion*, a daily paper pledged to support the Government and co-owned by Jorge Batlle who ran for President in November but subsequently promised his support to Bordaberry.

On 25 February the Argentine newspapers reported the capture by the police of an important Tupamaro, Hector Amodio Perez, and at least eight other Tupamaros. On the same day there was also a report of the kidnapping by the Tupamaros of a police photographer, Nelson Bardesio, reputed to hold the files of photographs of wanted men.

This latest kidnapping brought the number of important figures held by the Tupamaros – apart from Geoffrey Jackson and Ferrés who have been released – to four. The first two, Presidential Adviser Ulyses Pereyra Reverbel and the ex-Minister of Agriculture Carlos Frick Davies, have been held for over a year.

During March there were constant reports in the Argentine press of Tupamaro activities, some successful, some abortive. The new government was confirmed in office and harsher, more repressive measures were instituted. In a gun battle between police and Tupamaros four police and eight Tupamaros were killed.

On 13 April a general strike practically paralysed the whole of Uruguay. This had been called by the National Workers Convention in protest at the 'mockery' of a 20 per cent wage rise authorized by the government.

Likewise on 13 April the Argentine press reported that the previous day there had been a 'New and Spectacular Escape of Tupamaros'. In fact fifteen men escaped from the notorious prison Punta Carretas, from which one hundred and six Tupamaros escaped on 6 September 1971. Since that massive escape security had been tightened at the prison and an alarm system installed. However, the openings to the sewers had not been wired despite warnings from the firm installing the system that these presented vulnerable points. The men escaped by this route, mining the sewers behind them and setting booby traps at manhole covers so that the police were thwarted in their attempts to follow or intercept the escapees.

On 15 April the Uruguayan Government announced that a 'state of war" existed within the country.

On 18 April *La Prensa* reported a tragic shooting incident in Montevideo when seven civilians were killed and several more injured in a gun battle outside the Communist headquarters. Police and soldiers attacked the offices of the Communist Party and witnesses said that the shooting was entirely unprovoked, although official reports claimed that one of the persons shot had drawn a gun.

The same paper reported that strict press censorship was enforced in Uruguay and that only reports from official sources could be printed or broadcast. Copies of the paper were confiscated as they carried reports other than those officially authorized.

General comments in the press drew attention to the fact that although the Communist Party and the Tupamaros were known to be opposed to each other, this latest attack by the government could well lead all groups dedicated to changing conditions in Uruguay to sink their differences and fight together. Such a move could cause the government great embarrassment.

On 27 April *La Prensa* reported that the President of the Chamber of Deputies of Uruguay, Hector Gutierrez Ruiz, a very important personage indeed, had been kidnapped by the Tupamaros and held for twenty-four hours. He was seized outside his house and taken to the People's Prison where talks went on for over seven hours. Whilst there he was requested to interrogate Nelson Bardesio, the police photographer. Bardesio confessed to being a member of the police 'Death Squad', adding that many prominent members of the police and armed forces belong to this parapolice organization.

News of Gutierrez Ruiz' capture was reluctantly released and caused great consternation in government circles. When interviewed Senor Gutierrez Ruiz would not say whether or not he brought a message from the leaders of the Tupamaros, but did say that he felt the Tupamaros were a 'political' problem.

In the meantime the search-and-destroy operations by bands of police and soldiers were going on, especially in Montevideo where the death of two 'extremists' and the capture of at least ten others were reported. A priest, who had been arrested on 18 April after the search of a printer's shop 'Pax Romana', was later released. He had been accused of being in league with the Tupamaros, but the hierarchy of the Catholic Church in Uruguay declared their support for him and said they were convinced of his innocence.

On 29 April *La Prensa* carried an article more hopeful than anything emanating from Uruguay in past months. Although the Tupamaros were not specifically mentioned, it appeared that the Uruguayan Government was about to abandon its harsh stand and seek the cooperation of the opposition parties. Significantly, the article also stated that it had been agreed that General Pacheco, the ex-President and prominent member of Bordaberry's government, be appointed Ambassador to Spain (a-time-honoured method of removing from the scene a man important but embarrassing). The nationalization of private banks and agrarian reform were also mentioned.

Whether this apparent change of heart was in any way due to the talks between the kidnapped Gutierrez Ruiz and the Tupamaros can only be guessed, If matters really do improve in Uruguay the victory will undoubtedly belong to the Tupamaros. We can only wait and see – and hope. *we could use some Tupamaros in Amerika!*